HACKED

Kali Linux and Wireless Hacking Ultimate Guide with Security and Penetration Testing Tools, Practical Step by Step Computer Hacking Book

Alan T. Norman

Disclaimer Notice:
Please not the information contained within this document is for educational and entertainment purposes only. Every attempt has been made to provide accurate, up to date and reliable complete information. No warranties of any kind are expressed or implied. By reading this document, the reader agrees that under no circumstances are is the author responsible for any losses, direct or indirect, which are incurred as a result of the issue of information contained within this document, including, but not limited to errors, omissions, or inaccuracies

TABLE OF CONTENTS

Introduction

Chapter 1. Kali Linux

Chapter 2. Building a Hacking Environment

Chapter 3. Kali Linux External Boot Drive

Chapter 4. Essential Linux Terminal Commands

Chapter 5. Network Basics

Chapter 6. Tor and the Dark Web

Chapter 7. Proxies and Proxychains

Chapter 8. Virtual Private Networks

Chapter 9. Introduction to Wireless Networking

Chapter 10. Wireless Hacking Setup and Tools

Chapter 11. Hacking WPA2 Wi-Fi Encryption

Chapter 12. Wireless Routers and Network Exploitation

Chapter 13. Wireless denial of service

Chapter 14. Conclusion

INTRODUCTION

This book is intended to serve as an intermediate-level guide to some common penetration testing tools and skills – particularly those of wireless hacking and of maintaining anonymity. The material follows from the basic introductory information provided in the book **Hacking for Beginners (mybook.to/hacking-beginners)**, so it assumes that the reader has some familiarity with beginner hacking concepts and terminology. In contrast to **Hacking for Beginners**, this book concentrates more on practical execution, and provides some step-by-step procedures for installing essential platforms and tools, as well as the theory behind some basic attacks.

THE "BIG FOUR"

There are four main focus areas that all hackers should consider and finely hone, no matter what their level of competency. If you want to become a master hacker, you should be constantly working on improving yourself in all four of these areas. These "big four" are knowledge, tools, skills, and judgment. While reading this book and putting its ideas into practice, you should ask yourself which of these areas are relevant to the concept at hand. This will help you create a framework for your abilities and track your progress as you go along.

KNOWLEDGE

Deep and broad knowledge of relevant concepts is the foundation for any successful hacker. Gaining knowledge is not just the beginning of a hacking career, but must be constantly maintained because of how fast information grows and changes in the computer world. There is a seemingly unending supply of sources of knowledge and areas of study, so much so that it's likely impossible to know everything available. However, dedication to the constant pursuit of knowledge is essential. There are several areas to focus on that are critical for a working knowledge base in computer security and exploitation. In successive order, generally, they are:

- Computer and network architecture
- Networking protocols
- Information and network security
- Computer programming
- Data encryption
- Software and hardware vulnerabilities
- Anonymization
- Exploitation

These knowledge areas overlap in some instances and the reader is certainly not limited to the above list (the more knowledge, the better!), but it represents a good, starting "to do" list for self-studiers to begin.
Information in all these areas can be found in books,

ebooks, journals, websites, online and off-line courses, personal mentors, and conferences, among other sources. It can be helpful, if affordable, to become degreed or certified in networking, programming, or information security.

TOOLS

Knowledge is useless without the tools to exploit it. The hacker needs a basic set of hardware and software tools that remain basically the same regardless of skill level. These tools will accumulate and evolve over time, however, along with advances in technology and defense. The three basic categories of tools needed by a successful hacker are:

- A hardware platform such as a laptop or desktop computer, or mobile device
- Networking devices such as interface cards and wireless adapters
- Software such as operating systems (including virtual machines), development kits, network monitoring applications, and exploitation scripts and packages

Most of the tools are not particularly sophisticated, expensive, or difficult to obtain. Computers can be expensive, but most hacker operations don't require the latest and fastest machine on the market. For most procedures, a laptop computer that has a reasonable amount of memory and that can support modern operating systems is usually sufficient. Although most computers come standard with networking hardware, Wi-Fi penetration requires a special type of wireless chipset (see chapter 10) that typically doesn't come with standard adapters. An external USB adapter with this feature can be obtained relatively cheaply, however.

Almost all of the software needed for most common hacking procedures is free, open-source, and easily obtained. These tools are available openly for download and are updated frequently. Most of these tools are supported by a rich community of enthusiastic users that are an excellent resource for tips and troubleshooting. It is important for hackers to keep their software updated with the latest versions and patches and to monitor the community for current problems, solutions, and use-cases.

SKILLS

Hacker skills are gained when knowledge and tools are put together to achieve a purpose. At the end of the day, the skills of a hacker determine what he can or cannot accomplish. Once one has knowledge and tools, building a good skill set requires one thing... practice.

Skills can be practiced safely in a self-contained environment such as a local area network or personal area network, or in a set of networked virtual machines within a single system. In addition, there are a number of websites, both free and for-pay, where hackers and security professionals can practice offensive and defensive methods in a consequence-free space.

Like any other skill, hacking skills will diminish if not used, either with practice or application, on a regular basis. In addition, you can never assume that once a skill is learned that it remains a usable skill forever. The nature of hacking and security is such that it constantly and rapidly evolves. There was a time, for example, when SQL injection was a simple and common attack on websites – but now that administrators have caught on (and server-side code has become more secure) it is considered old-hat. A recent vulnerability in Wi-Fi networks has been discovered (see Chapter 11) that is now on the cutting edge. Skills must be refreshed with the latest knowledge and tools in order to remain effective.

JUDGMENT

Finally, and perhaps most importantly, a hacker must always practice sound judgment. While skills determine what a hacker *can* do, judgment determines what they *should* do. Much of the knowledge and skills required for hacking involve understanding multiple advanced concepts. Although modern society is very technically savvy, most people that you encounter in daily life don't have a fraction of the knowledge required to understand, much less execute, even the simplest of hacks. This puts hackers in a fairly exclusive club, giving the novice an intoxicating feeling of power and invincibility. Along with all of the technical knowledge that comes with the study of hacking however, should also come an understanding of the various risks and consequences. It is tempting to want to jump in feet first, and practice your newfound skills, but all actions should first be tempered with sober questions.

A hacker should have clear goals in mind before embarking on any endeavor, even those only intended for practice. All actions should be undertaken with due consideration of one's own ethical standards, community expectations, and potential consequences (see the dilemma in Figure 1). A common mistake for beginners is to overestimate their level of anonymity. An even graver error is to overestimate your level of skill. A poorly executed attack can reveal the hacker's identity or cause unintended damage or data loss in a target system. It takes time to reach an appropriate level of proficiency and competency for any task, and impatience can ruin everything.

Figure 1 - The hacker's dilemma

A FEW WORDS OF CAUTION

Before embarking on any penetration testing missions, or otherwise implementing the knowledge and skills gained from this book, the reader should keep the following cautionary advice in mind.

THE RAPIDLY CHANGING LANDSCAPE

More than any other type of industry or technology, the world of computers and information networks (in terms of both hardware and software) is a rapidly changing one. New versions – sometimes even several versions ahead - are always in production before the most current ones even hit the market. It is not usually possible to predict when a new version, sub-version, or patch will be released for any given package – or what changes will come with that release. The world of open-source software, where the majority of hacker tools come from, is especially chaotic. Versioning, patching, and documentation are often conducted by the user community and are not necessarily centrally maintained with any sort of rigorous quality control. There are several flavors of distributions for open-source operating systems and other tools, and they don't always coordinate changes to their base code. As a result of this rapidly changing and often unpredictable landscape, any given individual steps or command syntax for a particular procedure are subject to change at any moment. Furthermore, the implementation of certain procedures can differ, sometimes in subtle ways and sometimes drastically, depending on the nature of the hardware or operating system on which they are running.

This book attempts to outline the most recent, most common, and most universal information, and it provides caveats where procedures are known to differ. However, the reader should be prepared for the fact that there is often a great deal of troubleshooting and refining of individual steps that comes along with implementing many of the procedures introduced in this book. When errors or unexpected results occur, there are freely available resources on the Internet for getting up-to-date information. The best places to check are the host websites for the software in question, and various online hacker or software message boards. In most cases, someone else has already found and published a solution to the problem you are having.

THE LIMITS OF ANONYMITY

This book discusses several different tools and methods for hackers (or even just casual internet users) to maintain a degree of anonymity. These procedures range from hiding or obfuscating one's IP or MAC address to accessing resources through encrypted or multi-hop channels. However, it is important to understand that the nature of communication makes it virtually impossible for anyone to maintain 100 percent anonymity. A motivated and well-funded party, whether a criminal or a government organization (or both, in some cases) can very often determine the information that they are seeking. In many cases, it only takes a single, minor mistake on the part of the person wishing to remain anonymous to reveal their location or identity. The nature of the activities of that person will usually determine the resources others are willing to dedicate to finding them. It is still possible to maintain a high degree of confidence in one's anonymity by properly implementing several methods simultaneously. In many cases, this will make the time it takes to track someone down prohibitive and expensive. The bottom line is that you should never assume you are completely safe or anonymous.

LEGAL AND ETHICAL RAMIFICATIONS

Hacking for Beginners presents a detailed analysis of

the various legal and ethical issues that should be considered before undertaking computer hacking as a hobby or career. This book presents information in a matter-of-fact way, and encourages the user to use the knowledge gained with care and diligence. None of the tools or procedures outlined in this book are illegal or even unethical when used in the proper context. In fact, they are crucial for understanding the nature of modern information security threats and protecting against them. Furthermore, it is common and advisable to conduct attacks against one's own systems to identify and correct vulnerabilities. Attempting to access or compromise a system without permission of the owner is not recommended, especially for inexperienced beginners, and could lead to serious consequences, including criminal prosecution. Be sure to understand the laws and penalties - which can vary by country and locality - and, as mentioned above, don't count on anonymity to protect you.

CHAPTER 1. KALI LINUX

To get started with wireless hacking, one must first become familiar with the tools of the trade. No single tool is more valuable, especially to a beginning hacker, than Kali Linux. A free, stable, well-maintained, and astonishingly complete set of analysis and penetration software, Kali evolved in the crucible of open-source Linux distributions and has emerged as the king of all hacker operating systems. This successor to the notorious BackTrack distribution has everything that a hacker needs, from newbies to hardened experts.

A BRIEF HISTORY OF UNIX AND LINUX

In the early 1970's, the **Unix** – shortened from UNICS (UNiplexed Information and Computing Service) – **operating system** (OS) evolved from a defunct project by AT&T Bell Labs to provide simultaneous user access to mainframe computer services. As Unix became more formalized and grew in popularity, it began to replace the native operating systems on some common mainframe platforms. Originally written in **assembly** language, the rewriting of Unix in the **C** programming language enhanced its portability. Eventually, several versions of Unix, including ones for microcomputers, emerged in the commercial market. Several popular OS derivatives, referred to as *"Unix-like"* took shape in the following decades, including Apple's **Mac OS**, Sun Microsystem's **Solaris**, and **BSD** (Berkeley Software Distribution).

Efforts to create a freely available version of Unix began in the 1980's with the **GNU** ("GNU's Not Unix") General Public License (**GPL**) project, but failed to produce a viable system. This led Finnish programmer Linus Torvalds to tackle development of a novel Unix **kernel** (the core control module of an OS) as a student project. Using the Unix-like educational operating system **Minix**, Torvalds successfully coded an OS kernel in 1991, making the source code freely available for public download and manipulation under the GNU GPL. The project was eventually named **Linux** (a combination of Torvalds' first name, "Linus", with "Unix").

Although the term Linux initially referred solely to the kernel developed by Torvalds, it eventually came to designate any OS package that was based around the Linux kernel. Being an **open-source** effort, various Linux distributions evolved over the decades with unique sets of software libraries, hardware drivers, and user interfaces. The flexibility and efficiency of Linux led to widespread adoption by computing enthusiasts and some large organizations, both as a cost-saving measure and to circumvent the monopoly on operating systems by Microsoft.

Since most popular consumer and business software is

written for Microsoft and Apple platforms, Linux has never had the ubiquity or commercial appeal of Windows and Macintosh PC Operating Systems. However, the flexibility, portability, and open-source nature of Linux make it ideal for the creation of lightweight, highly customized distributions that serve very specific purposes. These distributions are typically built from the kernel up – only installing the minimum libraries and components necessary to achieve the purposes of the host hardware. This approach produces OS packages that use minimal memory, storage, and processor resources and have fewer security vulnerabilities. Linux, and the Unix syntax and structure on which it is based, is an essential part of a modern hacker's toolkit and knowledge base.

Hundreds of individual commercial and open-source Linux distributions have emerged and currently run on everything from small personal devices such as phones and smart watches, to personal computers, mainframe servers and military hardware. Most of these distributions have branched off from a handful of earlier Linux packages, including **Debian**, **Red Hat**, and **SLS**.

DEBIAN LINUX AND KNOPPIX

Debian, one of the earliest open Linux distribution projects, was consciously created to remain free and open while still maintaining high standards of quality.

Debian has had several major distribution releases of its own in addition to dozens of spinoff projects that use the Debian kernel and library base. Where two of these projects, **Linspire** and **Ubuntu** (a very popular distribution) were primarily aimed at home PC users, the **Knoppix** project was designed to be run live from an external medium, such as a CD-ROM. This - along with its ability to interface with a large array of hardware - made Knoppix an ideal tool for troubleshooting, data rescue, password recovery, and other utility operations. Knoppix was a natural base from which to develop the various security, **penetration testing**, and forensic sub-distributions that have been subsequently spawned.

BACKTRACK LINUX

Two Debian Knoppix-based distributions that focused on penetration testing were **WHAX** (previously **Whoppix**) and the **Auditor Security Collection**. Both projects ran on live CD's and featured a large repository of penetration testing tools. WHAX and Auditor Security eventually merged into the notorious distribution known as **BackTrack**.

KALI LINUX

The comprehensive offensive and defensive security suite included in BackTrack Linux made it the tool of choice for hobbyists, security professionals, legitimate penetration testers, and black hat hackers alike. The developer of BackTrack, Offensive Security, eventually rewrote the distribution, renaming the project as ***Kali*** Linux. Kali installation packages and virtual machine images are available free of charge. Offensive Security also offers for-pay courses in security using Kali, as well as professional certifications and an online penetration testing environment.

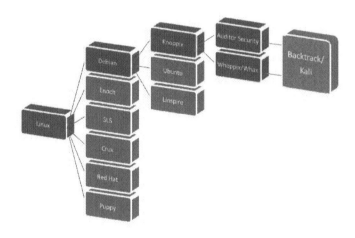

Figure 2 - Evolution of Kali Linux

KALI TOOLS

The centerpiece of Kali Linux, and the primary reason for its popularity among hackers and security professionals, is its extensive and well-organized suite of free tools. Kali currently features over 300 tools including passive information gathering, vulnerability assessment, forensics, password cracking, network analysis, wireless hacking, and a powerful set of exploitation tools. Although all of the tools included with Kali are free and open source and can be downloaded and built onto most (Debian-based) Linux derivatives - having a tested, vetted OS that comes native with such a large array of tools is an invaluable resource.

Among the most useful tools that come with Kali are:

Metasploit Framework – Metasploit is a popular vulnerability exploitation platform containing various analysis and penetration tools. It features multiple options for user interface and provides the user with the ability to attack nearly any operating system. Kali also contains *Armitage*, a graphical management platform that helps the user organize the operations and interactions between multiple Metasploit tools during an attack.

Wireshark – Wireshark is a multi-platform real-time network traffic analysis tool. All traffic on a chosen network node is captured and broken down into useful packet metadata, including header, routing information, and payload. Wireshark can be used to detect and analyze network security events and to troubleshoot network failures.

John the Ripper – John the Ripper is a legendary password cracking tool containing multiple password attack algorithms. Although originally written exclusively for Unix, John the Ripper is now available on several OS platforms. One of its most useful features is its ability to automatically detect the password encryption "*hash*" type. The free version of John the Ripper available on Kali supports the cracking of many password hash algorithms, but not as many as its commercial counterpart.

Nmap – Nmap, short for network map or network mapper, is a common hacking tool that is essential for penetration testing. Nmap allows the user to scan a network for all connected hosts and network services, providing a detailed view of the network's structure and members. Additionally, Nmap provides a list of each host's installed operating system as well as its open ports. This allows the user to zero in on known vulnerabilities during exploitation.

Aircrack-ng - Aircrack-ng is the quintessential software package for wireless analysis and penetration testing, focusing on Wired Equivalent Privacy (*WEP*), Wi-Fi Protected Access (*WPA*) and *WPA2-PSK* Wi-Fi encryption protocols. This tool features wireless packet sniffing, packet injection, wireless network analysis, and encrypted password cracking tools. Aircrack-ng requires network interface hardware that supports *monitor mode* functionality. Kali also features a more graphically-based wireless hacking tool known as *Fern*.

BurpSuite – BurpSuite is a collection of tools that focus

on the exploitation of web applications. These programs interact to not only test applications for vulnerabilities, but also to launch attacks.

The list above is by no means a complete one, but it is a representative sample of the power and flexibility that Kali Linux provides as a platform for penetration testing and for computer security in general. Kali can be run live from optical or USB media, as a standalone OS on a desktop or laptop workstation, as an alternative in a multiboot system, or within a virtual machine inside another host OS. The following chapter describes how install and configure Kali on various operating systems to create a proper environment for hacking and penetration testing.

Chapter 2. Building a Hacking Environment

In order to begin wireless hacking, one must first set up a proper environment for their tools, beginning, of course, with the installation of Kali Linux. There are three chief categories for installation of Kali Linux, depending on the needs and hardware of the user:

1) Hardware installation
   a. Standalone
   b. Dual/Multi-boot
2) Virtual installation
3) External media installation

Each type of installation has its own pros and cons, and the best choice depends mostly on the intended use of the software. Kali was not written to be an "everyday" consumer product with the typical software enjoyed by casual users, so installing it as a standalone OS on a personal computer is only practical if that particular machine will be dedicated to penetration testing activities. Alternatively, Kali can reside on the hard drive in a dual-boot or multi-boot scenario with other OS installations if space permits. Often, Kali Linux is installed within virtualization software inside of another OS, be it Linux or otherwise. This arrangement consumes more resources, but affords the hacker some more flexibility and allows him to practice attacks on other virtual machines within the host. Kali can also be used as a bootable "live" OS when installed on an removable external medium such as a CD-ROM or USB flash drive. Since optical disk readers are becoming exceedingly less common, a USB medium is more practical for external installations. An advantage of a live distribution is that it can be used on multiple machines and some of the digital forensic tools included with Kali Linux are best run outside of the boot structure of a target machine. This chapter will focus on the hardware and virtual installation procedures.

INSTALLING KALI LINUX ON A HARD DRIVE

The latest versions of Kali Linux have the following minimum requirements for a host machine:

1) 10 GB Hard Drive (20 GB recommended)
2) 512 MB RAM (1 GB recommended)

The user will also need either a USB port or a CD-ROM drive to boot the installation. It is recommended that the host machine have some sort of network interface, of course, for software updates and for connectivity in penetration testing efforts.

Whether installing Kali Linux as a standalone OS or in a multi-boot scheme, the first step in installation is to obtain the latest ISO (International Standards

Organization compliant disk image) from Offensive Security and copy it to an external medium. A list of the latest releases can be found at

www.kali.org/downloads/

It is recommended that ISO images be obtained from the developer, and not from a third party or file-sharing source, to ensure the integrity of the code.

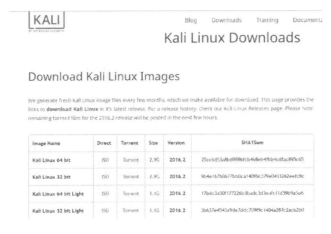

Figure 3 - Kali Linux ISO Download Page (2/2/17)

The ISO is available in 32 bit and 64 bit versions depending on the processor architecture of the host machine. Note that the 64 bit version will not run on a 32 bit processor. You can download the ISO directly from the corresponding link or through the torrent link if you have torrent client. An **SHA1Sum** hash is given for each ISO file. Once the file has been downloaded, its hash can be read using **checksum** software and compared to the given string. If the strings do not precisely match, then the file is compromised and should not be used. This checksum procedure guards against corrupted downloads or ones that have been hijacked (no honor among thieves!).

After downloading the desired Kali Linux version, burn it to a CD-ROM or copy it to a bootable USB flash drive (follow the instructions in section X for creating a bootable flash drive.)

STANDALONE INSTALLATION

Before beginning a standalone Kali Linux installation, it is important to understand that the procedure will **overwrite all existing data on the host drive**. This includes the previously existing OS, if any, as well as any other files or software.

The steps for a standalone installation are as follows:

1) Ensure minimum hardware and chip architecture

Check that your host machine meets the minimum hardware requirements for Kali (currently 10 GB storage and 512 MB RAM) and that it can support a 64 bit installation (if not, use the 32 bit version).

2) Back up any files on the host hard drive

Since the installation will overwrite any existing data on

the host hard drive, transfer or back up any needed files or settings (i.e. to a cloud drive, flash drive, CD, DVD, or external HDD).

3) Ensure proper boot order

Restart your host machine and enter the BIOS menu. Navigate to the boot order section (the menus will vary from computer to computer) and ensure that either your optical (CD/DVD/BR) drive or USB ports, depending on your chosen medium, is first on the list. The boot order can be changed to another setting, if desired, after installation. Be sure to save BIOS settings upon exiting the BIOS menu.

4) Load the ISO

After altering the BIOS, completely shut down the host machine, insert the optical or USB medium that contains the ISO, then power the computer back on. It may take a few moments for the Kali boot menu to appear.

5) Follow the installation instructions

When the Kali boot menu appears, select the **Graphical Install** option.

Figure 4 - Kali Linux Boot Menu

The following installation steps include general recommended options for beginning users of Kali. In most instances, the recommended options are already highlighted by default on each menu screen. These steps assume that your host machine has a live network connection – a menu may appear for wireless or wired network setup. If you do not have a network connection, there may be slight differences in your menu options. Note that this part of the procedure will be nearly identical for the multi-boot and virtual installations.

I. **Select a language** >> [Select your desired language]
II. **Select your location** >> [Select your location]
III. **Configure the keyboard** >> [Select your desired keyboard]

(Kali configures the network, which may take a few moments)

IV. **Configure the network** >> [use the default Hostname "kali" or choose your own]
   o **Domain name** >> [this can be left blank if not required by your network]
V. **Set up users and passwords**
   o **Root password**>> [choose a "root" (administrator) password]
   o **Non-root user real name** >> [choose an identification name for your non-privileged user account]
   o **Non-root username** >> [choose a username for your non-privileged user account]
   o **Non-root password** >> [choose a password for your non-privileged user account]

VI. **Configure the clock** >> [choose your time zone]

VII. **Partition disks** >> ["Guided – use entire disk"] >> [Choose the install hard drive for your host machine] >> ["All files in one partition"] >> ["Finish partitioning and write changes to disk"]
   o **Write the changes to disks?** [Yes]

(Kali installs... may take several minutes)

VIII. **Configure the package manager**
   o **Use a network mirror?** >> [Yes]
   o **HTTP proxy information** >> [Enter your proxy or leave blank]

(Kali configures... several minutes)

IX. **Install the GRUB boot loader on the hard disk**

- o **Install the GRUB boot loader to the master boot record** >> [Yes]
- o **Device for boot loader installation** >> [Choose the install hard drive for your host machine]

(Kali installs... several minutes)

X. **Finish the installation** >> [Continue]

(Kali installs... several minutes)

After installation, Kali will reboot your machine automatically. If your computer boots to the original boot menu screen (Figure 4), shut down the machine, remove the installation CD or flash drive, then power up again.

MULTI-BOOT INSTALLATION

Adding Kali Linux as a boot option on a computer with one or more existing operating systems requires allocation of separate hard drive space. Note that **incorrectly manipulating drive partitions can lead to loss of data**, and should be performed with care. It is recommended to back up files and data before manipulating partitions. Since every OS has its own disk management utility (in addition to some available third-party software), you should refer to the instructions for partitioning space on your native OS.

1. On the hard drive which you will be installing Kali Linux as a boot option, allocate a new 20 GB (recommended) partition using your current

OS's disk management utility or other disk utility software.

2. Follow steps 1-4 from the previous section to begin installation of Kali on an external medium.

3. Begin step 5 from the previous section, stopping before the "Partition disks" sub-step (5.VII).

4. Choose the "Manual" partitioning option and continue.

5. In the list of partitions on the next screen, highlight the partition created for Kali in step 1 above. **Be certain to only select the partition intended for Kali, or other data will be erased.** Continue.

6. In the "Partition settings" list, select "Delete the partition" and continue.

7. The next screen should now indicate the intended Kali partition as having "FREE SPACE". Select that partition again and continue.

8. On the "How to use the free space" screen, select "Automatically partition the free space" and continue.

9. For "Partitioning scheme", select "All files in one partition" and continue.

10. Finally, select "Finish partitioning and write changes to disk", continue, and select "Yes" to confirm writing changes. Continue, and resume installation at step 5.VIII.

Installing Kali Linux on a Virtual Machine

Advances in processor speed, the advent of multicore and multiprocessor chips, increased memory size, and increased data storage have made hardware virtualization a viable and practical means of running multiple software platforms on a single computing device. Running operation systems within a VM has advantages because it eliminates the need for multiple pieces of expensive hardware and makes the use of highly specialized distributions such as Kali practical. In addition, using penetration testing software within a single host allows hackers to practice attacks in a safe "sandbox" environment, targeting various other VM's within the host. The downside of using an OS within a VM is that there is competition for host resources, and the virtual hardware capabilities are limited to those of the host machine.

Functional and feature-rich virtual machine software is available free of charge. The most common free VM applications are ***Virtualbox*** and ***VMware Player*** (which has commercial versions with additional features). ***QEMU*** is an open-source option that runs solely on Linux. This book will use Virtualbox to demonstrate a virtual Kali installation because it is available for Windows, Macintosh, Linux, and even Sun systems.

INSTALLING THE VIRTUALIZATION SOFTWARE

Virtualbox is a popular multi-platform, open-source virtual machine application. The installation procedure is as follows:

1. Ensure minimum specifications

Virtualbox is designed to run on *x86* (Intel or AMD chips, et al) architectures and it is recommended that the host machine have at least 1 GB of RAM. Additionally, the host machine should have enough free hard drive space to accommodate any virtual machine OS's you intend to install.

2. Enable hardware virtualization

If you are using a Windows or Linux host computer, restart your and enter the BIOS menu. Navigate to the virtualization option (the menus will vary from computer to computer) and ensure that its enabled. Be sure to save BIOS settings upon exiting the BIOS menu.

Macintosh hardware does not use BIOS in the same manner as "PC" computers. Hardware virtualization, if not already enabled, must be set via command line in the terminal application. This is an advanced procedure requiring root access, and the command syntax may vary between Mac OS versions. Consult your documentation or manufacturer for enabling virtualization on Macintosh hardware.

3. Download installation files

The latest source code and binary distributions can be obtained at (Figure 5):

https://www.virtualbox.org/wiki/Downloads

Figure 5 - Virtualbox Download Page

Windows

The "Windows hosts" link provides an .exe binary Windows installation file. Documentation on the Virtualbox website lists the supported Windows versions of the current release.

Macintosh OS X

The "OS X hosts" link provides a .dwg Mac OS X disk image file.

Linux

The "Linux distributions" link launches a new page

listing various Virtualbox packages for different Linux distributions. However, it is recommended that you download and install Virtualbox through the package repositories on your individual Linux distribution (see step 4)

4. Install Virtualbox

Windows

Opening the Windows executable installation file will launch a typical Windows installation "wizard" dialog. Follow the installation instructions. The installation options and additional application choices depend on your individual preferences.

Macintosh OS X

Opening the .dwg disk image will mount the image and open a window containing the Virtualbox ".mpkg" OS X installation file. Launch the .mpkg file to begin installation and follow the instructions. The installation options and additional application choices depend on your individual preferences.

Linux (Debian-derived)

Most modern Linux distributions are derivatives of the original Debian and Fedora (e.g. Red Hat) kernels. To illustrate installation of Virtualbox on a Linux OS, the following steps describe the installation as it applies to an Ubuntu Linux (A Debian derivative) system.

Installation for other Linux distributions may vary in syntax and in repository locations. These steps should apply to most up-to-date Debian releases.

To install Virtualbox from an Ubuntu repository using the software center:

I.   Open the "Ubuntu Software" application from the launcher menu.
II. Type "virtualbox" into the search line at the top. VirtualBox should appear in the resulting package list (Figure 6).

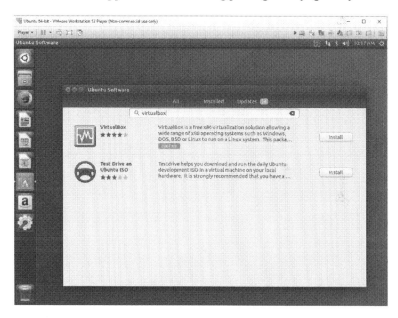

Figure 6 - VirtualBox in the Ubuntu Software Center

III. Click "Install" next to the VirtualBox package.
IV. If asked, enter your password to authenticate root access.
V.   Installation will proceed automatically for a short period.

To install VirtualBox from an Ubuntu repository using the command line:

    I.   Open the Ubuntu command line console, named "Terminal".

    II.   Type the following to update the software repository (enter root password if asked):

```
# sudo apt-get update
# sudo apt-get install virtualbox
```

    III.   Installation will proceed automatically for a short period.

INSTALLING THE KALI LINUX VIRTUAL MACHINE FROM A DISK OR ISO

Once the virtualization software is installed, Kali Linux can be installed on the host as a virtual machine. This example will once again feature VirtualBox to illustrate the procedure:

    I.   Open VirtualBox on your host machine.

    II.   Click "New" to create a new VM.

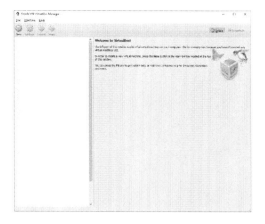

Figure 7 - Virtualbox Main Screen

III.   Follow the "Create Virtual Machine" wizard dialog, using the recommended parameters listed below:

      a. **Name and operating system**
          Name >> [Kali Linux] (or whatever you choose)
          Type >> [Linux]
          Version >> [Debian (64-bit)] (32 bit if applicable)
      b. **Memory size** >> [1024 MB]
      c. **Hard disk** >> [Create a virtual hard disk now]
      d. **Hard disk file type** >> [VDI (VirtualBox Disk Image)]
      e. **Storage on physical hard disk** >> [Dynamically Allocated]
      f. **File location and size** – use the default hard disk file name provided. It is recommended to allocate 10 GB – 20 GB for the virtual drive.

IV.   The Kali virtual machine you created will now appear in the list of VM's on the VirtualBox main window. With the

Kali VM highlighted, click the "Settings" button in the toolbar to launch the settings dialog.

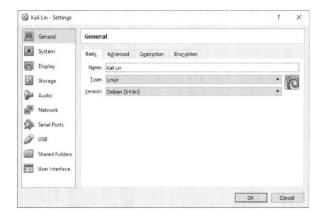

Figure 8 - Virtualbox General Settings

V. Set the following recommended settings by navigating through the settings menu options and tabs (change other options as desired):

    a. **System >> Processor >> Processor (s) >>** [2 or more]

    b. **System >> Processor >> Extended Features >>** [Enable PAE/NX]

VI. In the "Storage" settings, highlight the "Empty" IDE controller disk icon in the Storage Tree. Under "Attributes", Click the "Optical Drive" disk icon and navigate to the location of the Kali Linux .iso file downloaded at the beginning of this chapter. Click "Ok" to save and close the settings.

38

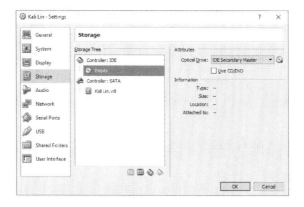

Figure 9 - Virtualbox Storage Settings

VII.   On the VirtualBox main window, with the Kali VM highlighted, click start to launch the VM.

VIII.   A new window will open, booting to Kali's initial boot screen. Follow the graphical install instructions given in the installation steps earlier in this chapter. On step 5.IX, "Install the GRUB boot loader on the hard disk", be sure to select the virtual Kali Linux drive created during the VM Installation. Complete the remainder of the installation steps.

INSTALLING A PRE-CONFIGURED KALI LINUX VIRTUAL MACHINE

Some OS virtual machines are available preconfigured for a particular virtualization application. These are known as **appliances** and allow the user to circumvent a great deal of setup work. To install a Kali appliance on VirtualBox, follow these steps:

I.   Go to the Offensive Security download page:

www.kali.org/downloads/

and click on "Kali Virtual Images".

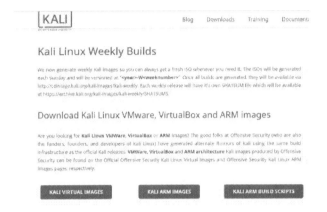

Figure 10 - Kali Linux VM Downloads

II.   Download "Kali Linux 64 bit VM" (or 32 bit if necessary for your hardware). Unzip the contents of the downloaded file to your desired directory.

III.   Open VirtualBox and choose "Import Appliance" from the file menu.

Figure 11 - Add Virtualbox Appliance

IV. Navigate to the directory containing the ".vbox" file and select your desired appliance.

V.   Click "Next" to get to the Settings page and make any desired changes, then click "Import". This will complete the VM installation.

Chapter 3. Kali Linux External Boot Drive

One of the advantages of Linux operating systems is that each distribution is built from the kernel up with only the packages and applications needed or desired for the purposes of each particular release. This has resulted in extremely "lightweight" (i.e. small build size), yet fully functional distributions. The original purpose of developing small distributions was to meet the need for fully functioning "live" operating systems to run from external media with limited space, such as CD-ROMS and USB flash drives, and to make efficient use of resources on some older computing platforms. Flash drives have since exploded in capacity along with processing power, but it has still become a bit of a competition and a point of pride among Linux developers – both amateur and professional – to see how small they can shrink a functional Linux distribution. Some distributions are as low as 12 MB in size.

Aside from the drive capacity and performance considerations, however, it is often desired to boot Linux from external media for functional reasons. This is particularly true of Debian/Knoppix-derived distributions whose purpose is to provide utility or security functions for multiple machines. Data recovery, password resets, and forensic functions often need to be performed outside the boot sectors of the machines in question, making it necessary to boot the tools on separate media. Furthermore, specialized distributions such as Kali don't necessarily serve well as primary, standalone operating systems for everyday use, so booting from an external medium as needed from a desired machine is often more practical. This chapter describes how to create a bootable USB flash drive for Kali Linux. This drive can be used as a live-running OS or as an installation source.

CREATING A BOOT DRIVE FROM WINDOWS

The Offensive Security website contains detailed instructions on creating a live Kali boot drive on various operating systems. The instructions can be found at:

http://docs.kali.org/downloading/kali-linux-live-usb-install

This section will summarize the instructions for Windows, and provide some additional suggestions.

WIN32 DISK IMAGER

The Win32 Disk Imager program embeds a raw disk image onto a removable device. It can be downloaded free from the link on **Sourceforge** below as well as from other free software repositories on the Internet.

To install a Kali image using Win32 Disk Imager, follow these steps:

1. Download the Win32 Disk Imager installation file and follow the installation wizard procedure.
2. Insert the USB or CD-ROM that you would like to use as a boot medium.
3. Launch the Win32 Disk Imager program. Note that your machine may require administrative privileges to run this software.

4. Under the "Image File" box, navigate to the location of your Kali Linux .iso file.

Figure 12 - Win32 Disk Imager

5. Under "Device", select the drive letter corresponding to the destination medium. **Be sure to choose the correct medium, as subsequent steps will overwrite all data!**
6. Click "Write" to complete the procedure.

YUMI

The Win32 Disk Imager is simple and useful. For more flexibility, however, the Yumi Multi-boot software is another option for creating a live Kali USB drive. Yumi is freely available, along with instructions, on the Pendrivelinux website:

https://www.pendrivelinux.com/yumi-multiboot-usb-creator/

Yumi can be used to create bootable media with single or multiple distribution options. Upon booting, a Yumi medium will display the boot options in a menu.

To install a Kali image using Yumi, follow these steps:

1. Download the Yumi installation file.
2. Insert the USB or CD-ROM that you would like to use as a boot medium.
3. Launch Yumi (there is no install procedure, Yumi runs directly as an .exe).
4. Under "Select the Drive Letter of your USB Device", choose the drive letter corresponding to the destination USB drive. **Be sure to choose the correct medium, as subsequent steps will overwrite all data!**

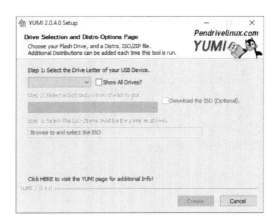

Figure 13 - Yumi Main Screen

5. Under the "Select a Distribution to put on…" box, choose Kali (look under "System Tools"). Kali Linux .iso file.
6. Under "Browse and Select your kali *.iso" box, navigate to the location of your Kali Linux .iso file.
7. Click "Create" to complete the procedure.

CREATING A BOOT DRIVE FROM OS X OR LINUX

Creating a boot disk from a Linux or OS X platform requires advanced command-line instructions. It is recommended that you refer to the Offensive Security website (below) for up-to-date instructions on creating a live Kali medium.

http://docs.kali.org/downloading/kali-linux-live-usb-install

CHAPTER 4. ESSENTIAL LINUX TERMINAL COMMANDS

Before the emergence of graphical user interfaces and ergonomic input devices such as mice, computer users had only their keyboard and a monochromatic screen with a prompt. Commands were entered line-by-line and either interpreted on the spot or compiled *en masse* into a program. In order to interact with the file system or peripherals (via the kernel), users had to employ a lexicon of special commands to perform desired actions. The original Unix systems, in fact, booted directly to a command terminal (typically a login prompt) to await input. Although most modern Linux distributions now boot to a GUI, the operating system is still underlied by the Unix terminal command system. Any Linux system can be made to boot directly into the command line, but most users open the **Terminal** application from the main GUI desktop if they want to enter commands directly.

Although "point and click" graphical interfaces are convenient and generally more intuitive, advanced Linux users - especially hackers - often prefer to use the terminal to execute commands. Typing a Linux command manually is not only, in many cases, more efficient, but it also gives the user more direct control over operations. A single, one line command, entered properly, can replace multiple clicks and nested windows. Furthermore, by entering a command directly, the user can more easily trace the source of errors. Hackers tend to be independent, self-reliant individuals, and are loathe to relinquish control of their machine to automated processes written by others.

This chapter will discuss how to navigate in Linux through the Terminal, and introduce some of the more critical shell commands.

LINUX SYSTEM ANATOMY

Before getting into the command list, it is important to understand the basic structure and file system of a typical Linux distribution. The command library is very powerful and can control virtually any aspect of the operation or configuration of a Linux system.

ARCHITECTURE

All Linux systems are built upward from the kernel. The kernel is the machine-level instruction set that loads into memory when the OS is booted. Kernel instructions interact directly with the machine's hardware, including the processor(s), memory, network interface, and any peripherals.

The Linux shell (Figure 14) is the means by which a user interacts with the kernel. The shell can be either a direct command prompt or a graphical user interface.

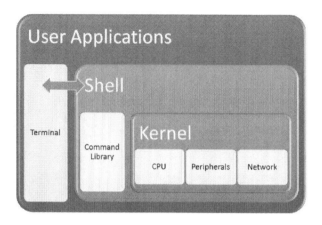

Figure 14 - Linux Kernel Architecture

THE DIRECTORY SYSTEM

Linux has an organized directory structure that is designed to compartmentalize files for security and stability. Directory paths use the fore-slash (/) to separate subsequent directory names in the path, as opposed to Windows which uses the backslash (\ ). The term "root" can at times be confusing to Linux beginners because there are a few locations which may be referred to as a root directory. The true "root" in a Linux file system – inasmuch as there are no parent directories above it – is designated simply by a lone fore-slash, "/". All other directories lie under this location. The directories under "/" vary slightly between Linux distributions, but the general structure was inherited from the original Unix system and is largely universal.

Figure 15 - Linux Directory Structure

LINUX COMMANDS

Linux has a rich set of terminal commands, many of which are the same, or similar, to those of the original Unix OS. These commands allow users to manage and manipulate files and folders, install software, interface with peripherals, and among many other tasks, perform various networking operations. Although Linux commands will be introduced in context in various sections throughout this book, the following basic commands serve as an introduction to the basic Linux lexicon and the general format and usage of terminal commands.

DIRECTORIES AND FILES

The first commands a Linux user should learn are the ones associated with navigating and manipulating directories. Once at the terminal command prompt, the following command will list the files and directory present in the root directory:

```
# ls
```

In most cases, the default terminal directory will be '/home/username', so typing "ls" will list the contents of the current user's files and folders.

```
user@UbuntuVM: ~
user@UbuntuVM:~$ ls
Desktop    Downloads        Music     Public     Videos
Documents  examples.desktop Pictures  Templates
user@UbuntuVM:~$ 
```

Most Linux commands feature options that can be appended to the default command form. These options vary for each command, and range from changing the format of the output to directing the command to perform specific functions that it doesn't perform by default. The "-l" option for the ls command is an example of a command option that results in more detailed output.

```
user@UbuntuVM: ~
user@UbuntuVM:~$ ls -l
total 44
drwxr-xr-x 2 user user 4096 Jul 29 10:15 Desktop
drwxr-xr-x 2 user user 4096 Jul 29 10:15 Documents
drwxr-xr-x 2 user user 4096 Jul 29 10:15 Downloads
-rw-r--r-- 1 user user 8980 Jul 29 10:13 examples.desktop
drwxr-xr-x 2 user user 4096 Jul 29 10:15 Music
drwxr-xr-x 2 user user 4096 Jul 29 10:15 Pictures
drwxr-xr-x 2 user user 4096 Jul 29 10:15 Public
drwxr-xr-x 2 user user 4096 Jul 29 10:15 Templates
drwxr-xr-x 2 user user 4096 Jul 29 10:15 Videos
user@UbuntuVM:~$ 
```

Note that the directory listing now contains details for each file and folder in the current directory, including access permissions, size, and creation date. Options are preceded by various symbols (-, --, |, etc.) depending on the nature of the command ans option. Many options can be chained together in a single command, making them a powerful way to accomplish many things in an efficient single line of code.

51

To display the options for a particular command, along with other useful information, one can append the command with "-- help". However, the help output for mot commands is several pages long and cannot be viewed in a terminal window without scrolling. Attaching the "| more" option will pause after a single page of output, allowing the user to advance page-by-page by pressing the spacebar until the output is complete.

```
user@UbuntuVM: ~
user@UbuntuVM:~$ ls --help |more
Usage: ls [OPTION]... [FILE]...
List information about the FILEs (the current directory by default).
Sort entries alphabetically if none of -cftuvSUX nor --sort is specified.

Mandatory arguments to long options are mandatory for short options too.
  -a, --all                  do not ignore entries starting with .
  -A, --almost-all           do not list implied . and ..
      --author               with -l, print the author of each file
  -b, --escape               print C-style escapes for nongraphic characters
      --block-size=SIZE      scale sizes by SIZE before printing them; e.g.,
                               '--block-size=M' prints sizes in units of
                               1,048,576 bytes; see SIZE format below
  -B, --ignore-backups       do not list implied entries ending with ~
  -c                         with -lt: sort by, and show, ctime (time of last
                               modification of file status information);
                               with -l: show ctime and sort by name;
                               otherwise: sort by ctime, newest first
  -C                         list entries by columns
      --color[=WHEN]         colorize the output; WHEN can be 'always' (default
                               if omitted), 'auto', or 'never'; more info below
  -d, --directory            list directories themselves, not their contents
  -D, --dired                generate output designed for Emacs' dired mode
  -f                         do not sort, enable -aU, disable -ls --color
--More--
```

The cd command allows the user to change the active directory to a specified location. A given path is assumed to be relative to the current directory unless otherwise constructed. To change to a directory within the current active path, simply append cd with that directory name. Note that Linux file and directory names are case sensitive.

```
user@UbuntuVM: ~/Desktop
user@UbuntuVM:~$ ls
Desktop     Downloads              Music      Public      Videos
Documents   examples.desktop       Pictures   Templates
user@UbuntuVM:~$ cd Desktop
user@UbuntuVM:~/Desktop$
```

To switch to a path that is not in the active directory, the absolute path must be specified.

```
user@UbuntuVM: ~/Documents
user@UbuntuVM:~$ ls
Desktop     Downloads              Music      Public      Videos
Documents   examples.desktop       Pictures   Templates
user@UbuntuVM:~$ cd Desktop
user@UbuntuVM:~/Desktop$ cd /home/user/Documents
user@UbuntuVM:~/Documents$
```

The following is a short list of useful Linux directory and file commands. It is by no means a complete list, but represents some of the most common commands. Care must be taken with some of these commands, because they may change or delete the contents or location of a file or folder.

Command	Action
pwd	Displays the path of the active directory
ls	Displays the contents of the active directory
cd	Changes the active directory
mkdir	Creates a new directory
rmdir	Deletes a directory (if empty)
cp	Copy a file
mv	Move a file
rm	Delete a file

"SUPERUSER" ACCESS: THE SUDO COMMAND

One more important Linux command is the infamous "sudo" command – one every aspiring hacker should know. The term "sudo" is (reportedly) short for "superuser do" and indicates to the kernel that the subsequent command is to be executed with root access (or sometimes as a user different from the one who is currently logged in).

```
user@UbuntuVM:~$ cd /home/user2/Documents
user@UbuntuVM:/home/user2/Documents$ ls -l
total 4
-rw-rw-r-- 1 user2 user2 5 Jul 29 12:13 passwords
user@UbuntuVM:/home/user2/Documents$ rm passwords
rm: remove write-protected regular file 'passwords'? y
rm: cannot remove 'passwords': Permission denied
user@UbuntuVM:/home/user2/Documents$ sudo rm passwords
[sudo] password for user:
user@UbuntuVM:/home/user2/Documents$ ls -l
total 0
user@UbuntuVM:/home/user2/Documents$
```

Above, a user navigated to the Documents folder of another user, but was denied permission to delete a file, named "passwords". When the command was reissued using sudo, the user was prompted for a password, and then the rm command was successfully executed.

CHAPTER 5. NETWORK BASICS

The most straightforward way, of course, to gain access to a particular system would be directly from the interface terminal of the target device. This presents many obstacles to the hacker because it requires him to gain physical access to the system, exposing him to being discovered or leaving traces of his presence. However, the networked nature of most computers and information technology provides safer, less conspicuous avenues to exploitation – the network.

In general, a network is any collection of interconnected parts. There are networks of people, organizations, political states, machines, and just about any group of entities in which information passes between members. Computer and IT networks have grown and combined to connect billions of nodes, from small household networks with one or two personal computing devices to enormous server farms that require their own powerplants.

Whether sending contact information from one smartphone to another with a bluetooth connection, or streaming a movie through the internet from Moscow to Buenos Aires, the basics of networking and communication are the same. Understanding computer networking and communication protocols is essential to becoming an effective hacker.

Network Components and Architecture

All it takes is a minimum of two computing devices connected in some way as to share information, and you have a computer network (Figure 16). Any device capable of some sort of connectivity can comprise a node on a network. Traditional user platforms like servers, desktop PCs, laptops, tablets, and personal handheld devices such as smartphones are common on networks. There are also an increasing number of networked peripherals and standalone smart appliances like printers, televisions, gaming platforms, network cameras, entertainment consoles, audio devices and watches. Each device can typically connect to multiple other devices through various communication media. Physical connections like copper wiring and fiber optic cable serve as a backbone to the global internet, and connect most networks up to the main access point of a local area network. Within a LAN, any number of connection types may exist, including physical wiring and Wi-Fi. At short ranges, devices may connect through Bluetooth or Near-Field Communication (NFC) technology. Alongside of this architecture is a growing broadband cellular network that consists of any array of radio-frequency towers that are connected to the Internet backbone and to various satellites. As broadband cellular technology improves, usage is expanding beyond telephones and are becoming the primary internet access methodology for many individual devices and small networks.

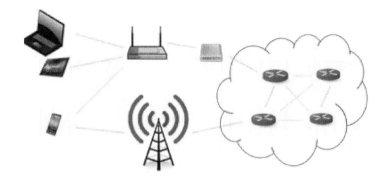

Figure 16 - Network Components

NETWORK MODELS AND PROTOCOLS

Regardless of the type of node or communication medium, two devices must communicate using some sort of common protocol. A standard protocol used by all devices across a network is necessary to prevent miscommunication. Internet Protocol (IP) had been around since the earliest days of networking. Although it has changed a bit in form and function, it remains the de facto standard for network communication. IP, combined with another standard known as Transmission Control Protocol (TCP) forms a layered networking paradigm called TCP/IP. This scheme divides a network into various layers from the basic network hardware up to the user application. The collection of protocols is a conceptual network communication model known as the TCP/IP model, or TCP/IP "stack". There is another model known as the Open Systems Interconnection (OSI) model, which is more granular with regard to the number of layers. The OSI model can be more generally applied, but it describes the same essential principles as the TCP/IP model.

THE TCP/IP MODEL

The TCP/IP model consists of four, stacked, conceptual layers that each have a role to play in the preparation and transport of data from one point in a network to another. These are the application, transport, network, and data link (or link) layers.

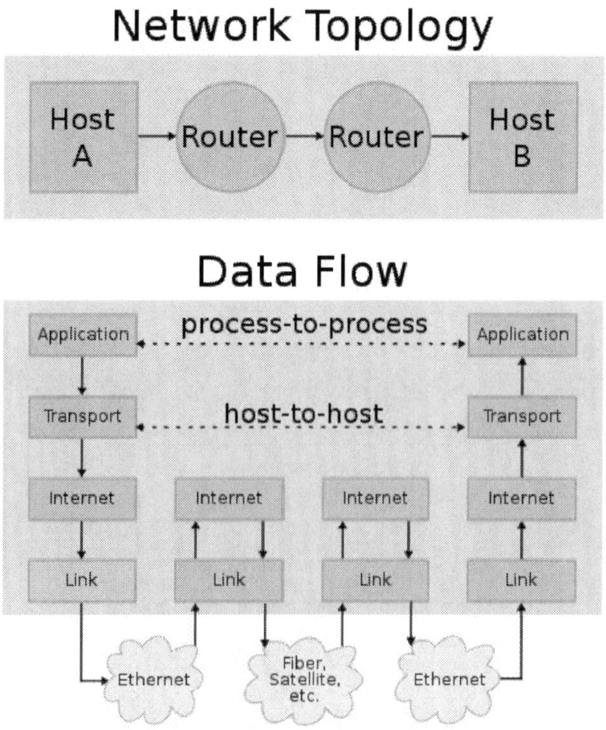

Figure 17 - Network Data Flow in Layers (infosecinstitute.com)

58

The application layer of the TCP/IP stack (considered the "top" layer) is the layer most visible and accessible to the user. This is the layer where the content or payload of a communication is created before it is packetized for transport. Email clients, web browsers, file sharing software, video streaming applications and other connected apps all operate in the application layer. It's worth noting that the application layer executes other protocols that reside within (or above) TCP/IP. This includes the hypertext transfer protocol (HTTP) of web applications, smtp for email, and File Transfer Protocol (FTP) among others.

Functioning in the transport layer is an advanced concept, but suffice it to say that this layer helps to ensure the quality of communication through error checking and other means. Additionally, the transport layer is where information passed from an application is initially divided into packets, which are then appended with appropriate headers. TCP operates at this level, but it is not the only protocol available. User datagram protocol, or UDP is used when it is necessary to sacrifice the successful arrival of a small number of packets in exchange for real-time delivery of information. UDP is the transport protocol of choice for audio and video streaming.

The network layer, often called the Internet layer, is where the work of routing packets is done. In this layer, the best network route for a packet is determined, then the packet header is appended with a source and destination IP address before it is relayed to the network interface hardware. There are other protocols that can operate at this layer, but IP is by far the most prevalent, and is the underlying structure for most global data communication. The manipulation of IP headers at various stages of transit is the basis for many hacking attacks.

The bottom layer of the TCP/IP model is the hardware or data link layer. The hardware layer is the last stop of a data packet before it leaves its source machine and arrives at its next destination through the physical medium. The MAC addresses of the network hardware involved in relaying the packet are appended to the packet header at this level.

NETWORK PROTOCOLS

When one node in a network communicates with another, it divides its message into small, independent packets. Each packet is then appended with a header as it passes through each layer so it can be properly reassembled into a message at its destination. The beauty of TCP/IP is that each individual packet may take a different route, and can be resent if lost, assuring a high degree of efficiency and message fidelity.

At the heart of TCP/IP is the IP address. Each device on a network has a unique address to identify its location within the network and any subnetworks to which it belongs. Understanding IP addressing because it allows them to zero in on particular targets. In addition, hackers may need to hide or manipulate their own IP address in order to remain conspicuous.

The standard version of IP has been IP v.4 for many years and is used on most networks and devices. IP v.6 is a new standard that can accommodate many more addresses. Within an individual LAN, the first octet in an IP address typically indicates the designation of the overarching network, with subsequent octets designating subnetworks and individual machines.

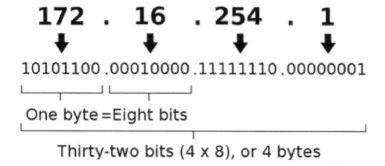

Figure 18 - IP Address Notation

One of the most important things to understand about IP addressing is that the IP address of a given node within a local network is different than the one assigned to it when it communicates through the Internet. This is because it's impossible to control or prevent two individual machines on separated networks from accidentally or intentionally being given the same address.

From the hacker's perspective, IP addresses provide a roadmap on any individual network to identify and distinguish individual machines. Additionally, so much tax involved intercepting individual data package in transit on the network. The header information in the packet contains the IP address of birth the source and the destination. It is the manipulation of these headers that allows doctors to conduct man in the middle and denial of service attacks. It is the manipulation of these headers that allows knockers to conduct man in the middle and denial of service attacks.

IP addresses are considered logical addresses, meaning they are assigned via software, either directly by the user or automatically through some kind of process. IP addresses reside on the network layer. In many cases, IP addresses can be spoofed or forged in a packet header. This can be done to obfuscate the source of an email or some other attack payload, or to maliciously reroute packets.

It's important to understand that IP forging cannot be used to hide any two-way communication. In order for two machines to exchange information, their addresses must be valid or the packets being exchanged cannot reach their destinations. This is why it is futile to try to hide or change ones IP address when operating on a peer to peer service, or to hide the designation of a downloading node. The best one can hope for in this scenario is to route information through a large number of geographically and logically distinct proxies. The TOR network, which serves as a basis for the Dark Web, operates by creating multiple layers through which information can pass.

Another important type of device identifier is the (Media Access Control) MAC address. MAC addresses are considered permanent physical addresses and are assigned to individual network interface devices. The MAC addressing scheme is designed so that no two devices should, in theory, ever have the same designation. The address is burned into the device ROM so that it cannot be easily changed. MAC addresses are part of the data link layer.

Although MAC addresses are intended to be permanent, there are ways to "spoof" an address by writing a false address onto a packet header. This does not change the permanent address of a device, but allows a hacker to avoid being identified through their network interface. If an attacker with a spoofed MAC gains local access to a network, especially through wireless means, they can avoid being traced through their hardware.

DETERMINING NETWORK PARAMETERS

To find the IP address of a Linux machine, as well as the MAC addresses of any network interface devices, type

```
# ifconfig
```

into a terminal window. The current machine's IPv4 address on the local network is given in the "inet addr" field under the network adapter section (in this case "enp0s3"). The MAC address of the network adapter appears (in this case partially obscured) in the "HWaddr" field.

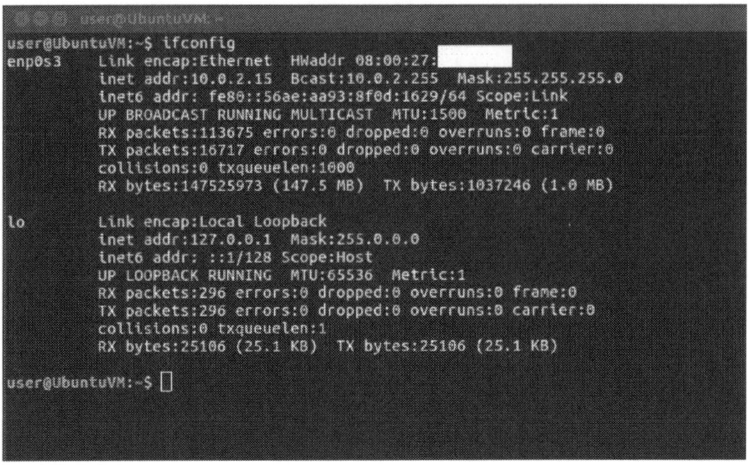

Figure 19 - ifconfig results

A useful Linux command for illustrating the path of a packet across the internet is **traceroute**. The traceroute command displays the IP address of each location, or "hop", that is used to relay a message from its origin to its destination. It also displays measurements of the time (in milliseconds) of a round trip between each hop and the subsequent hop. There are multiple options for a traceroute command, but the simplest demonstration is to run traceroute to a common destination. The destination can be entered as a Web URL or a known IP address. (Note, traceroute is native in Kali Linux, but if the command doesn't work in your Linux version it may need to be installed using the command:

```
# sudo apt install traceroute
```

Also, if you are using Linux in a virtual machine, it must be configured to use a bridged ethernet connection to the host machine's adapter, or traceroute won't function properly.) To trace a packet from the terminal source to a common, stable destination like Google (The equivalent command in a Windows terminal is **tracert**.):

```
# traceroute -q 1 google.com
```

The "-q 1" option limits each hop to one query for simpler faster output.

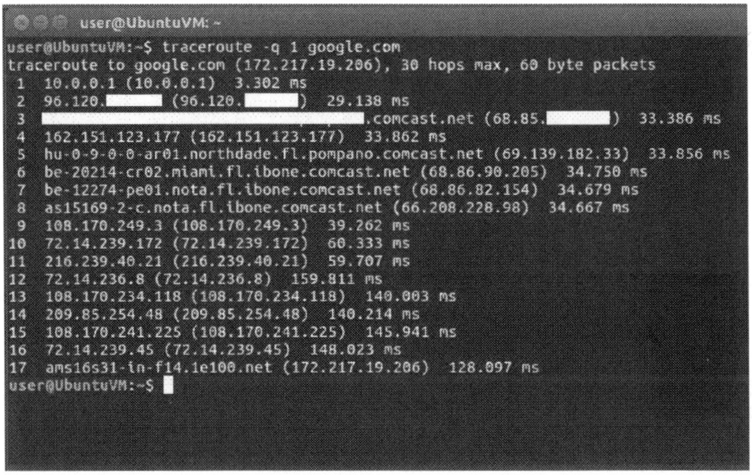

Figure 20 - traceroute results

The first location, 10.0.0.1, is the local IP address of the network router. The publicly-assigned IP of the origin does not appear on a traceroute. (You can find your IPv4 or IPv6 address through any number of websites. Simply typing something like "what's my ip" or "what's my ipv4" into a search engine will bring up multiple websites that will freely display your information.) The next IP in this example represents the first point of contact to the internet service provider (ISP). It can be seen how each subsequent hop travels through the infrastructure of the ISP until it reaches the internet backbone then moves along to its destination.

It is possible to map each IP address to a physical location using some online services. This can be used to create a map of hops from source to destination. These can be interesting and illustrative, but should be treated carefully because the information is not guaranteed to be accurate or up to date.

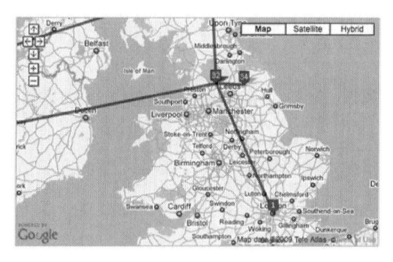

Figure 21 - Visual traceroute

The **ping** command can also be used to test the timing between source and destination, but without including the time between individual hops. The ping command is most often used to simply test the connectivity between nodes. The simplest way to "ping" is to simply type the command along with the destination URL or IP address:

```
user@UbuntuVM: ~
File Edit View Search Terminal Help
user@UbuntuVM:~$ ping google.com
PING google.com (216.58.212.238) 56(84) bytes of data.
64 bytes from ams16s22-in-f238.1e100.net (216.58.212.238): icmp_seq=1 t
tl=48 time=128 ms
64 bytes from ams16s22-in-f238.1e100.net (216.58.212.238): icmp_seq=2 t
tl=48 time=127 ms
64 bytes from ams16s22-in-f238.1e100.net (216.58.212.238): icmp_seq=3 t
tl=48 time=131 ms
64 bytes from ams16s22-in-f238.1e100.net (216.58.212.238): icmp_seq=4 t
tl=48 time=127 ms
64 bytes from ams16s22-in-f238.1e100.net (216.58.212.238): icmp_seq=5 t
tl=48 time=138 ms
64 bytes from ams16s22-in-f238.1e100.net (216.58.212.238): icmp_seq=6 t
tl=48 time=131 ms
64 bytes from ams16s22-in-f238.1e100.net (216.58.212.238): icmp_seq=7 t
tl=48 time=133 ms
^C
--- google.com ping statistics ---
7 packets transmitted, 7 received, 0% packet loss, time 6010ms
rtt min/avg/max/mdev = 127.199/131.226/138.841/3.748 ms
user@UbuntuVM:~$
```

Figure 22 - ping results

The program will ping indefinitely until it times out or until interrupted by the user (the "-c" switch limits the number of attempted pings to those specified.) Note that the output contains the IP address of the pinged URL. The ***ping6*** command can be used alternatively to determine a location's IPv6 address.

CHAPTER 6. TOR AND THE DARK WEB

The balance between privacy and security is a perpetual struggle, particularly in a world that is burgeoning with the both the spread of democracy and the existential threats of terrorism. This is further complicated by the cat-and-mouse game between authorities, criminals, and those who wish to remain anonymous online. Whether for simply protecting personal privacy, or for hiding nefarious activities, the desire for anonymous internet communication has resulted in several mechanisms being developed for that purpose. The Tor network is a popular system consisting of like-minded individuals that use open-source software to create a series of virtual connections between users. Used properly, the Tor network can significantly thwart efforts to trace communications traveling through it.

THE TOR SYSTEM

Tor is an acronym for "The Onion Router", referring to the layered nature of the network (like the layers of an onion), whereby a message is enveloped within multiple levels of encryption. The function of Tor essentially comes down to routing a message through multiple nodes in such a way as to resist attempts at traffic analysis. Before a message is sent, the source client builds a virtually random path, one hop at a time, through other participating nodes. Each node only knows the location of the nodes immediately preceding and subsequent to it because all other header information is encrypted with its own key. Once a path is established, secure traffic can begin between the source and destination. However, to maintain security, a new route is calculated every several minutes. The relays through which communications pass on Tor are servers run by volunteers across the globe.

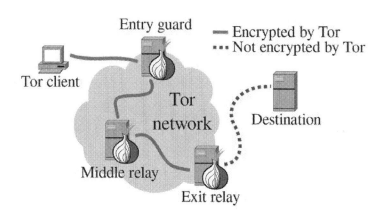

Figure 23 - The Tor Network

THE TOR BROWSER

The most common method of accessing the Tor network is through a Tor Browser. The Tor Browser is a modified version of the open source Mozilla Firefox (Extended Support Release version) web browser. The browser features several Firefox extensions along with the Tor proxy which establishes a connection to the Onion router. It is also configured by default not to save cookies and browsing histories.

The Tor Browser is free and can be downloaded and installed for Windows, Mac, and Linux platforms. There is also a mobile Tor app called Orbot that runs on Android devices. The browser can be downloaded from the Tor Project's main website.

https://www.torproject.org/projects/torbrowser.html. en

There are 32-bit and 64-bit versions available (only a 64-bit for Mac) in multiple languages, including the latest stable version and some experimental/beta releases.

Figure 24 - Tor Download Page

The Windows version is installed through a typical "wizard". If the host machine is behind a proxy or firewall, however, additional configuration steps may be necessary. For Mac, simply click the .dmg to extract, then drag the resulting app into the Applications folder.

The instructions for installing the Tor Browser on Linux platforms require some terminal commands and configuration steps that can vary between distributions. The Tor website has some general instructions, but there are specific steps (and often some troubleshooting) to get the browser to function properly on certain platforms, especially Kali Linux.

These additional steps can typically be easily found through an internet search or on the distribution home page. Some distributions may also have the Tor Browser available in their software repository that can be installed through the software installation application in the GUI of the OS.

THE DARK WEB

The "Dark Web" is a term that refers to the contents of the internet which are only accessible using anonymizing and routing protocols such as the Tor network (It is a common misconception that the Dark Web and the "Deep Web" are interchangeable terms, but "Deep Web" simply refers to the sites on the World Wide Web that are not indexed by search engines.) The anonymous nature of communication on the Dark Web is the source of a great deal of controversy worldwide because such anonymity eventually leads to the proliferation of objectionable, and sometimes dangerous, content. In addition to serving as a possible communication channel for terrorists, the Deep Web facilitates the open distribution of illegal narcotics, weapons, stolen financial information, and illicit pornography, among other things. However, the system also provides people living under repressive regimes their only access to certain kinds of information.

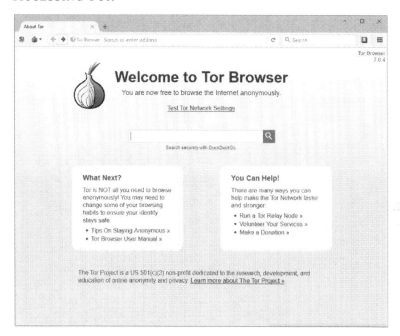

Figure 25 - Tor Browser Home Page

When launching the Tor Browser for the first time, it's a good idea to become a bit familiar with the system before jumping right into the Dark Web. It is advisable to read through the manual provided on the Tor Browser home page. In addition, Tor provides a link to some tips for properly using the system to maximize anonymity.

To check that the browser is properly connected to the Onion router, click "Test Tor Network Settings" on the default home page. The resulting page will report the IP address that websites see when you connect to them.

This is the address of the final node, or "exit node" of your current Tor circuit. To see the other nodes in your circuit, click the green "onion" icon (labeled "Tor Enabled" on hover) in the upper left corner of your browser. This will reveal the hops on the circuit. Every so often this path will automatically change, but you can change it manually by clicking "New Tor Circuit for this Site" on the same panel.

Figure 26 - Viewing the Tor Circuit

The exit node IP address that websites see for your connection is different from the public IP address assigned to your machine by your ISP. This is how you achieve anonymity. You can confirm this by going into a standard web browser (not on Tor) and checking your public IP address.

One thing to consider when using Tor is that many internet service providers attempt to detect whether their customers are using Tor, and either block traffic or report the activity to law enforcement. Although they cannot under most circumstances trace particular actions back to a user, the fact that Tor is being used can bring unwanted attention. The detection of Tor traffic can be circumvented, even if only temporarily, using Tor bridges or bridge relays. Because of the nature of Tor, Onion nodes are publicly known, so an ISP can see if a customer is connecting to a Tor entry point. Bridge relays are alternative entry nodes that attempt to remain obfuscated, but it must be noted that they are generally less reliable than public Tor nodes. Furthermore, some ISP's have still found ways to detect bridged connections by scrutinizing packets. Bridges also exist that support entities known as pluggable transports that obscure Tor activity from censors by alternating the traffic between the user and the entry bridge.

To set up the Tor Browser to use bridge relays, click the Onion drop-down menu icon and open the "Tor Network Settings" dialog.

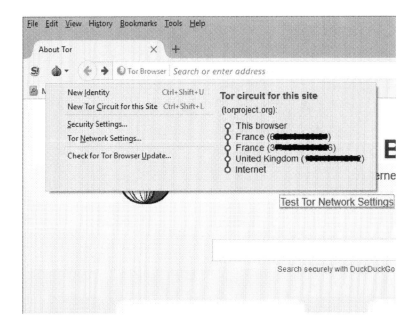

Figure 27 - Tor Settings Menu

Check the box next to "My Internet Service Provider (ISP) blocks connections to the Tor network" and choose the "Connect with provided bridges" radio button. Choosing the obs4 transport type will enact pluggable transports.

Figure 28 - Tor Settings Dialog

If you have your own list of bridge relays that you prefer to connect, choose the "Enter custom bridges" radio button and paste the bridge locations into the text box, one per line. A list of bridges can be found on the Tor Project website at the link below, but hackers should always be on the lookout for fresh bridges from trustworthy sources.

Standard bridges:

https://bridges.torproject.org/bridges

Pluggable transport bridges:

https://bridges.torproject.org/bridges?transport=obfs4

Figure 29 - Tor Bridge Settings

Tor is un underlying process that the Tor browser uses to access the Onion router, but it can also be used with other applications aside from a browser. This is especially important when running exploits. To set up Tor to use pluggable transport bridge relays on Linux without using the Tor Browser, some terminal commands and configuration are necessary.

Assuming Tor has already been installed, enter the following commands to download and install the obsf bridge services (use sudo if necessary):

```
# service tor stop
# apt-get update
# apt-get install obsfproxy obsf4proxy
```

Now open the "torcc" configuration file (under the /etc/tor/ directory) in a text editor. It's good practice to make a backup copy of the current file before making any changes. Insert the following text (## is simply a comment line), with the desired bridge locations after each line that begins with "Bridge". Save the file.

```
## Bridges
UseBridges 1
ClientTransportPlugin obfs3 exec /usr/bin/obfsproxy managed
ClientTransportPlugin obfs4 exec /usr/bin/obfs4proxy managed

Bridge obfs4 5████████████████████████████████████████
Bridge obfs4 13███████████████████████████████████████
Bridge obfs4 10███████████████████████████████████████
```

Start Tor from a terminal:

```
# service tor start
```

To confirm that tor is running, open a standard web browser (not the Tor Browser). In the network settings, set the Manual proxy configuration to a local SOCKSv5 host of 127.0.0.1:9050.

Figure 30 - Tor Browser Proxy Settings

Navigate to:

check.torproject.org

The site should confirm that Tor is connected. However, after this check, set the browser's network settings back to normal and only use the Tor Browser for web access. Now, when Tor is run from the terminal, other applications can be run with a bridged connection to the Onion network.

Figure 31 - Tor Connection Confirmation

Remember that simply connecting to the Tor network does not guarantee protection. In addition to using the Tor Browser (if using Tor for the Web), the Tor organization recommends certain practices to enhance anonymity:

1. Don't use torrent file sharing applications over Tor
2. Don't install any plugins into the Tor Browser or enable any that are disabled by default
3. Always use HTTPS URLs
4. Don't open downloaded documents from the Tor Browser
5. Use a Tor bridge relay when possible

TOR HIDDEN SERVICES

A few words of caution before we embark on a glimpse into the Deep Web. A great deal of the content available is not necessarily indexed, and the ones that are often expire quickly. The indexes that do exist contain an eclectic mix of sites with various content and services, many of which are illegal in most countries. Be certain that you understand the laws and penalties associated with any activity that you choose to engage in on the Deep Web. Furthermore, hackers and very powerful government agencies are constantly probing Tor for weaknesses, shutting down servers, and compromising nodes, so one's anonymity is by no means certain.

Although websites on the standard internet (known as the "clearnet") under traditional domains such as ".com", ".net", and ".org" can be accessed through Tor, there is a virtual domain known as ".onion" that can only be accessed anonymously via Tor. These locations, known as "hidden services" are the essence of the Dark Web.

One resource that lists various Dark Web hidden services is the "Hidden Wiki". There is not an official, centrally-managed Hidden Wiki, but rather it refers to several independent sites that attempt to index current hidden services of interest. A typical Hidden Wiki consists of multiple categories of links, some clearnet and some hidden, many of which have existed for a long time. Although Hidden Wiki editors try to keep up to date, the Dark Web is very dynamic, so sites come and go often or change URL's. Up-to-date Hidden Wiki's can usually be found using a search engine, and some exist on the clearnet, but the ones with .onion URL's can only be accessed through an Onion router (Note: there are ways to access hidden services without Tor, but not anonymously.)

Figure 32 - Tor Hidden Wiki

There are three types of search engines to be aware of with respect to Tor:

1. **Hidden-service-based engines that search the clearnet**: These are good for anonymously searching the Web. An example is "DuckDuckGo" (which also has a clearnet version), whose .onion domain can normally be found on a Hidden Wiki.

2. **Clearnet-based engines that search the Onion network**: An example is Ahima.fi. You

do not need to be on Tor to access this, but you will not be anonymous.

3. **Hidden-service-based engines that search the Onion network**: An example is "Torch", whose .onion domain is typically listed on a Hidden Wiki.

CHAPTER 7. PROXIES AND PROXYCHAINS

Although the ultimate goal of an attack is typically to gain access (get root!), deliver a payload, or disrupt a service, hackers of all sorts have little interest in getting caught. In many cases, the principal challenge is not the hack itself, but rather the process of hiding your identity and covering your tracks. If a packet arrives at a target machine with the IP address of the originator still embedded in the header, it takes minimal effort for security personnel to track down the perpetrator. Moreover, it does little good to spoof the originating IP (unless you're conducting some sort of denial-of-service attack) because you need to retrieve packets as well in most cases. To make it more difficult for investigators to track the origin IP of a user, it's useful to employ an intermediary known as a *proxy*. Properly stringing together multiple proxies, in fact, can make it exceedingly difficult for anyone to be tracked without a great deal of effort and expense.

PROXY SERVERS

The word "proxy" in English usage essentially means "representative". Just as someone might represent you and your interests at a meeting or legal proceeding, a *proxy server* relays communication from a source to a destination. However, the destination node will see the

IP address of the proxy server as the originating agent. When the proxy server receives packets back from the requested service, it relays them back to the requesting party. The originating IP address, although stored at the proxy location, is not included in the headers of packets traveling between the proxy and destination. This serves to obscure the identity of the originating party from the destination server.

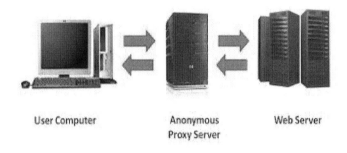

User Computer   Anonymous   Web Server
Proxy Server

Figure 33 - Proxy Server Configuration

Proxy servers are not just used for anonymity, however. Proxies are often employed as a protective barrier between a local network and the internet at large. Having a server as an intermediary can serve to filter information in both directions, preventing both incoming attacks as well as access to unauthorized outside resources.

TYPES OF PROXY SERVER IMPLEMENTATIONS

An important internet protocol in the application layer of the TCP/IP stack is SOCKet Secure, or **SOCKS**. SOCKS, in general, handles connection requests and packet transfers between clients, proxies, and servers. The SOCKS5 implementation supports additional security and authentication measures. *HTTP* proxies use the same headers and protocols to connect to web servers through the proxy as if it were a direct connection, making them more efficient for web use. The advantage of SOCKS implementations, however, is that they support additional protocols beyond HTTP. Note that Tor is itself a type of SOCKS proxy implementation.

PROXY SERVER USES

Organizations with internal networks often want to control the use of outside internet connections by their personnel. This is both to prevent individual users from inadvertently bringing compromising scripts into the network as well as to prevent them from accessing otherwise undesirable or non-work-related content like personal email, gaming, social media, video streaming, financial trading, or adult content. An internally administered web proxy can filter (either by white-listing or black-listing) content and block access to restricted locations, domains or services. Interestingly, employees can often circumvent these restrictions by accessing an outside proxy server. In fact, many proxies exist for this specific purpose. If the organization's firewall is not specifically blocking the IP address of a particular outside proxy server (this is why some choose to use white-listing) then it can relay content to a user through its own un-blocked IP address, thus bypassing the content filters.

Many users connect to proxy servers in order to access websites or servers anonymously. This could be just for general privacy reasons or to hide hacking activities. Sometimes users who have had their IP address banned from a website or an online service will attempt access through a proxy. Also, many countries block their inhabitants from accessing certain domains, or block outside parties from accessing local content. Proxies can be used to present the impression that one is in a particular geographic location to circumvent these restrictions.

Malicious proxy servers can be set up by hackers to lie between a target user and a legitimate location. If the target user is unaware of the arrangement, or is under the impression that they are using a safe proxy, the hacker can read and record traffic passing between the nodes or conduct man-in-the-middle attacks.

FINDING AND CONNECTING TO OPEN WEB PROXY SERVERS

The ability to use a proxy server for the purposes of anonymity depends in large part on the fact that the system being accessed is unaware that it is connected to a proxy. Services that do not wish users to connect to them via proxy will block any known proxy server IP addresses. As a result, the addresses of publicly available proxy servers are largely ephemeral. Users can find for-pay (and some free) proxy servers that use client-side software to update the proxy address as needed. Alternatively, users can check any number of websites that maintain regularly updated lists of known open proxy servers, so they can connect with a new server if the old one expires or gets blocked. These lists often contain the speed, reliability, host country, last known successful connection, and other information in addition to the server IP address and port of each server in sortable format. Some sites featuring open proxy lists are:

https://www.proxynova.com/proxy-server-list/

http://www.publicproxyservers.com/proxy/list1.html

http://list.proxylistplus.com/Fresh-HTTP-Proxy-List-1

Although some proxy servers are web-based, and will connect you to destination services within their own web application, it is usually necessary to configure a web browser or OS to connect to a desired proxy address.

In Windows 10, the proxy server can be set under Control Panel > Internet Options > Connections > LAN Settings.

In Linux, open the Network application and select the Network Proxy section. Choose the Manual configuration to enter the proxy address.

In Windows, Linux, and Mac, a proxy server can also be configured within the browser settings.

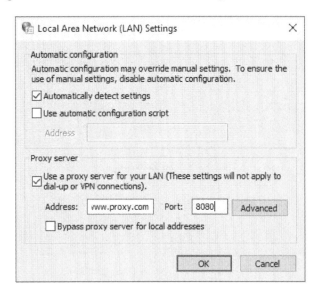

Figure 34 - Browser Proxy Settings

PROXYCHAINS

Although proxy servers do a sufficient job in most cases to hide a client's IP address from a destination server, they are only providing one layer of protection. Since the client's IP address is known – even if only temporarily – by the proxy server, that information could be obtained by accessing the proxy server logs.

Security personnel or hackers may try to obtain these logs through hacking of their own or through law enforcement subpoenas. However, each proxy server only has the IP address of the requesting party immediately preceding it. Thus, if multiple proxies are used it becomes increasingly difficult, expensive, and time-consuming to track the origin of a packet.

Proxychains is a simple but powerful Linux program that routes internet traffic through a series of proxy servers for the purpose of obscuring the identity of a client. Hackers often use Proxychains in conjunction with information gathering or exploitation programs to keep their location and identity secret. It should be reiterated here that no anonymity measures are completely foolproof, and Proxychains is no exception. Law enforcement and the hacking community are constantly looking for ways to compromise common hacking and anonymity tools.

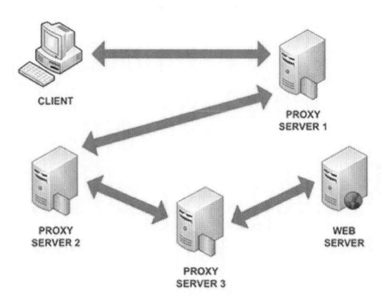

Figure 35 -A Proxy Chain

INSTALLING AND CONFIGURING PROXYCHAINS ON LINUX

Proxychains is a standard tool in the Kali Linux suite. To install in any Linux distribution:

```
# sudo apt-get install proxychains
```

The settings and proxy server lists for proxychains can be set in the configuration file, proxychains.conf, usually located in the /etc path. One of the choices a user needs to make is whether to set up a strict or dynamic proxy chain. A dynamic chain will maintain connectivity by skipping a server in the proxy list if it goes down. By default, the strict_chain option is enabled and dynamic_chain is commented out. To enable dynamic chaining, remove the comment hash (#) from the dynamic_chain line and type a new hash before strict_chain.

The [ProxyList] section of the configuration file is where you can put a line-by-line list of proxy servers to be used in the chain. The configuration file will have an example of the format required for each proxy line, which consists of the proxy type (HTTP, SOCKS5, etc.), address port, user name (if needed), and password (if needed), each separated by a space or tab:

```
socks5 192.168.67.78 1080 lamer secret
http   192.168.89.3   8080 justu hidden
socks4 192.168.1.49   1080
http   192.168.39.93 8080
```

A great thing about proxychains is that it can use Tor as a proxy source. In fact, by default, the proxychains configuration file is set up to access the local Tor port. However, you must check the configuration lines to ensure that all correct proxy types for Tor are included. If the [ProxyList] section only contains the following line,

```
socks4      127.0.0.1 9050
```

then it is set to use Tor, but only with SOCKS4 protocol, which may not work. Add the following line to ensure use of SOCKS5:

```
socks5      127.0.0.1 9050
```

Remember that to use proxychains through Tor, the Tor

service must first be running:

```
# service tor start
```

Now, to use a program through proxychains simply type proxychains followed by the program name and any desired option tags. To test the configuration, you can run a simple nmap (discussed later) scan on a safe website.

Figure 36 - Running proxychains

CHAPTER 8. VIRTUAL PRIVATE NETWORKS

The relay mechanisms of the previous two topics, Tor nodes and proxy servers, belong to a particular group of entities known as **exit nodes**. The purpose of an exit node, regardless of how it actually functions, is to face a destination server on behalf of a user, obscuring both the identity of the user and any subsequent pathways. Another popular type of exit node is the **virtual private network** (VPN). A VPN is essentially a means of extending a local network to external nodes so that those nodes become a part of the local network. This practice has many legitimate uses, including allowing corporate networks in disparate geographical areas to securely connect and share resources. Of course, it would be a great advantage to hackers to be able to join the network of a target server in this manner.

VPN'S AND TUNNELING

The power of a virtual private network lies in the practice of **tunneling**. Instead of connecting to a destination server through the internet via a service provider, the user establishes an encrypted connection to a VPN server which then connects to the destination. Although an ISP can see if a user is connected to a known VPN server IP address, it cannot read the encrypted traffic. When a request is sent from the user to the VPN server, the VPN service decrypts the request (which includes the destination headers) and relays it through the internet. When packets are sent back to the VPN, they are re-encrypted and relayed back to the user through the established tunnel.

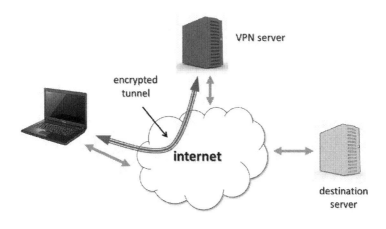

Figure 37 - A VPN Tunnel

VPN TYPES AND USES

There are two main types of VPN servers in terms of their purpose, **remote access** and **site-to-site**. A remote access VPN is the one most commonly used by home or personal users to either protect their anonymity or to bypass ISP, corporate, or regional access restrictions. Home or corporate users also can use this type of VPN to join their respective LANs from an outside location. This arrangement can be desirable for organizations with multiple locations or remote personnel who need to securely access central databases or services. Home users can set up a VPN in a similar manner to access their files at home or to remotely control their computer.

Although a remote access VPN can create an encrypted connection, it is done by encapsulating packets that are traveling through the internet just like standard traffic. Site-to-site VPNs create a more secure connection by employing protocols that maintain router-to-router communication. This communication is only possible after mutual authentication of the server and client.

VPN PROTOCOLS

The type of protocol used by a particular VPN service depends largely on the purpose of the server and the needs of the user. Many commercial VPN services will allow clients to select the type of server protocol they wish to use. This choice is often a trade-off between security, reliability, and speed. Encryption, by nature, will itself slow down connection speeds to a degree, but since multiple users are typically sharing access to a server, heavy congestion can further slow the speeds. The type of content being accessed also affects protocol choice. Video and audio streaming require UDP port support and greater bandwidth than simple HTTP browsing. Certain corporate connections may require support of certain file transfer protocols.

OpenVPN is an increasing popular VPN protocol that uses various open-source libraries for encryption and communication. The biggest advantage of OpenVPN is that it can be applied to virtually any port or sub-layer protocol. It is difficult for ISPs to block and it is considered the most reliable protocol, particularly in terms of security. One drawback is that most browsers do not currently support OpenVPN natively. In most cases it is necessary to use third-party software to connect a computer or a mobile device to a VPN server with this type of protocol.

Point-to-point tunneling protocol (PPTP) is an older VPN protocol which, although still widely used, is not generally recommended when other options are available. PPTP offers encryption, but it is replete with security vulnerabilities and can be more easily exploited than other protocols. However, because of its support of older platforms and legacy operating systems, in addition to its ease of use, it is still commonly found. Many VPN services will provide PPTP as an option for clients who need it, but will warn them of the security risks. This protocol is best suited for advanced users or in applications for which secure communication is not a top priority.

Layer 2 Tunneling Protocol (L2TP) is another VPN protocol that is often chosen for its ease-of-use and native support, but does not provide a highly secure channel. L2TP does not perform its own data encryption, so it must be combined with some other encryption protocol (usually Internet Protocol Security, or **IPsec**). Another drawback of L2TP is that it is confined to a particular port, making it relatively easy for firewalls or ISPs to block its use.

There are other protocols with newer types of encryption and different platform support, but OpenVPN, PPTP, and L2TP are some of the most common for consumer use.

CHOOSING A VPN

A home user looking to use a VPN for freedom, security, and anonymity when connecting to the internet have several choices, with the usual trade-offs between cost, speed, security, and reliability (i.e. stability). Although VPNs provide encryption and an exit node for clients to obfuscate their identities, users may want to know whether their activity is being logged. Free VPN services are available, but must be used with an abundance of caution.

USER LOGGING

One of the most important things to consider when choosing a VPN service is whether or not the provider maintains client connection and activity logs. If VPN activity logs are either subpoenaed by law enforcement or compromised by hackers, then the relative anonymity provided by the exit node is no longer an advantage. If a user wants an extra layer of anonymity, they should choose a "no logging" VPN service. It is important to note, however, that "no logging" really means *minimal* logging. There is a certain degree of internal logging that must occur during VPN operations in order to maintain connection speed and reliability, and to prevent attacks on the servers. The best services use just the minimum amount of logging necessary to maintain stable operations, and don't keep records of those logs any longer than necessary.

Users should be skeptical of a VPN, especially a free one, that claims not to log activity until they find out exactly what the service does and does not log (there are often caveats and "fine print" to no-logging claims). Furthermore, free VPN services may not necessarily be trustworthy themselves. Due diligence must be done before using a free VPN. It is helpful to look online for user reviews to see which services (both free and for-pay) are reputable.

ADDITIONAL *VPN SECURITY CONSIDERATIONS*

If a user is hesitant to purchase a subscription to a reputable VPN service for fear of losing their anonymity due to the transaction, there are several commercial VPNs that allow clients to pay with the anonymized digital currency of **bitcoin**.

If a user is concerned with having their identity revealed through VPN logs, even through "no logging" servers, it is possible for users to combine VPN connections by a process called **VPN chaining**. This can be accomplished by connecting to a VPN on a host machine, then setting up a different VPN service on a virtual machine within that same host. If any logs are compromised on the inner VPN, the activity will be logged as coming from the outer VPN. Of course there's nothing to stop someone from then trying to obtain the logs of the outer VPN, but it adds an additional obstacle and layer of anonymity. In theory, there is nothing preventing a user from creating multiple virtual machines within virtual machines, each with a different VPN, but each additional layer will significantly slow the connection speed. Even just a two-VPN chain can be very slow. Some commercial VPN services have an option for users to automatically chain two of their servers (which doesn't require setting up a virtual machine).

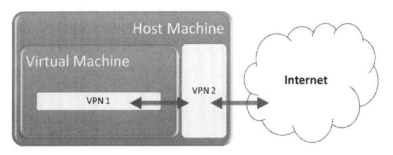

Figure 38 - VPN Chaining

101

Note that some VPN services also give users the option of connecting from the VPN server to the destination through the Onion network. Although this can provide additional security advantages, it also comes with a reduction in connection speed.

CHAPTER 9. INTRODUCTION TO WIRELESS NETWORKING

For the earliest years of computer networking, virtually all connections between nodes were made by copper cabling. Copper wire is efficient, durable, and inexpensive – plus it was copper that initially comprised the backbone of the internet (which was originally implemented on the existing telephone switching system). As broadband data needs increased, fiber optic media replaced copper for a large part of the internet backbone, but local networks remained mostly copper-based. The relatively recent explosion of mobile devices, along with the fact that laptop PC's began replacing less portable desktop units as primary computing devices, necessitated the widespread implementation of wireless networks.

Although more convenient and flexible than hard-wired networks, wireless networks are inherently less secure because the signals are broadcast in all directions instead of being confined to wires. The remedy for this vulnerability has been to encrypt communication between wireless nodes. Hackers who are able to break the encryption algorithm on a wireless network can then gain access to their desired target.

WIRELESS TECHNOLOGIES

There are several types of wireless communication standards that are generally distinguished by their purpose, range, bandwidth, and speed. Each of these standards is governed by their own set of protocols at the appropriate layers, but still operate under TCP/IP to relay information as part of a network. Because wireless signals are omnidirectional and spread out into the open air, the signal quality drops quickly as distance increases from the signal source, so data rates can only be maintained over a certain range. Additionally, wireless signals are subject to electromagnetic interference which can degrade signal quality.

Wireless Fidelity (**Wi-Fi**) is a ubiquitous wireless communication standard that is commonly used to implement both local and commercial LANs. Wi-Fi effective range is up to about 100 meters without obstruction or interference, but for most urban and residential environments the effective range for a reliable connection is about 10-30 meters. Bluetooth technology is typically applied to smaller devices and accessories within the confines of a personal area network (PAN) and can extend to about 10 meters. The short-range, Near-Field Communication (NFC) Standard is normally restricted to short-term data transfers within a range of 0.1 meters or less (at times requiring physical contact between devices). Figure 3 shows the approximate relative ranges of these standards on a logarithmic scale.

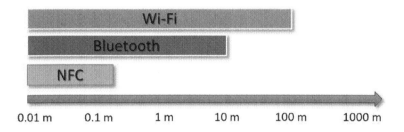

Figure 39 - Comparative Ranges of Wireless Network Standards

WI-FI NETWORKING

Wi-Fi is so common now that it is nearly impossible to find an area in any modern city where one does not detect either a public or private network signal. This, of course, is the heart of Wi-Fi's vulnerability – the fact that anyone in range can monitor the signals without being physically connected to the network or even, in some cases, on the intended site of the LAN. In fact, one method hackers have employed is to simply drive or walk down city streets (this is called *war-driving*) looking for unprotected Wi-Fi networks to exploit. Often, hackers would then mark these spots for other hackers to find by placing symbols on buildings or curbs using chalk. This practice is known as *war-chalking*. This vulnerability clearly makes the encryption of Wi-Fi networks imperative.

THE 802.11 STANDARD

The original standard for W-Fi communication was set by the Institute of Electrical and Electronics Engineers (IEEE) 802.11 standard. This standard has been amended over the years with various speed, range, and security updates. The 802.11g and 802.11n standards stood subsequently for several years until the recent release of 802.11ac (which will likely achieve its own obsolescence before long). Since higher frequencies support more bandwidth, the frequency bands supported by Wi-Fi include 900 MHz, 2.4 GHz, 3.6 GHz, 5 GHz, and 60 GHz (known as wireless gigabit, intended for high-speed audio and video applications). The bands currently used in most systems are the 2.4 GHz and 5 GHz bands, which are each segmented into several channels. Although lower frequencies carry less bandwidth, they are less susceptible to scattering by walls and other obstructions.

A Wi-Fi network, as defined by the standard, consists of two or more wireless **stations** whose communication is governed by a **coordination function** (CF). All stations governed by a single CF comprise the **basic service set** (BSS) of the Wi-Fi LAN (See Figure 4).

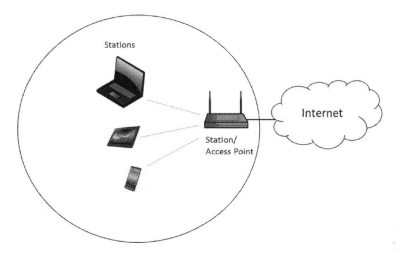

Figure 40 - Wi-Fi LAN BSS

Each station is expected to provide four basic services:

- **Authentication** – properly identifying a station on the network
- **Deauthentication** – voiding a previously authenticated station
- **Privacy** – encryption of message frames
- **MAC Service Data Unit (MSDU) Delivery** – delivering a data frame to its destination

A station that serves as a wireless **access point** (which is normally a Wi-Fi router) must deliver five additional services:

- **Association** – mapping an authenticated station to the access point
- **Disassociation** - voiding a previously associated station

- **Reassociation** – remapping a station to another access point
- **Distribution** – handling delivery of MSDU frames within the LAN
- **Integration** - handling delivery of MSDU frames between the LAN and an outside wired LAN

WI-FI NETWORK OPERATIONS

Parameters

A Wi-Fi network is defined by three basic parameters that distinguish it from other nearby networks: The network name, operating mode, and operating channel.

The network name is known as the service set identifier (**SSID**). Although routers come with a default SSID, most users change it to a desired network name. It is possible to suppress the broadcast of a network's SSID for privacy, but knowledgeable hackers can easily find hidden network names.

Wi-Fi networks can function in either **ad-hoc** or **infrastructure** operating modes. Infrastructure networks are the most common, as they consist of a central access point that services multiple client stations. This is how most home or business LANs are configured. An ad-hoc Wi-Fi network is simply a direct two-way connection between two stations (for instance between a computer and a wireless printer).

If there are multiple Wi-Fi networks within range of one

another, it is best that they operate on separate sub-frequencies (i.e. channels) within a common band. Each unique network can be assigned a channel manually, or can be configured to automatically switch channels to avoid overlap. Maintaining non-overlapping network channels can improve network performance for all BSS's in a given area.

Authentication and Handshakes

In order to maintain security and data integrity between two nodes in a wireless LAN, mutual authentication must first take place. Authentication is the process of confirming the identity of a station (including both clients and access points). In the context of authentication, a client is known as a **supplicant** and the AP is an **authenticator**.

These two parties must perform a four-way "**handshake**" to complete mutual authentication. The IEEE 802.1X standard describes the establishment and exchange of **cryptographic keys**. One example of this requires the use of a key that was shared between the two parties in advance and a concatenated key known as a pairwise transient key (PTK). Another important concept for hackers to understand is the **cryptographic nonce**. A nonce (short for "**non**sense" used "on**ce**") is simply a random value that is issued to be used one time and then discarded. The main purpose of a nonce is to ensure that handshake communications cannot be captured and used later by hackers to force authentication (known as a **replay attack**).

With these ideas in mind, a four-way handshake proceeds as follows (Figure 5):

1. The access point (AP) generates a nonce (ANonce) and sends it to the station (STA) to be authenticated.
2. The STA constructs the PTK from the pre-shared key, the received ANonce, its own nonce (SNonce), its own MAC address, and the AP MAC address. However, the only information it sends back to the AP is its SNonce and an algorithmically-generated message integrity code (MIC) to verify the authenticity of the message.
3. With the SNonce, the AP has all the information it needs to construct the same PTK that the STA constructed in the previous step. The AP then constructs an additional key called the group temporal key (GTK) – needed for multicast operations on the network – and sends it to the STA with a MIC.
4. Finally, the STA sends a standard acknowledgement (ACK) back to the AP, and the handshake is complete.

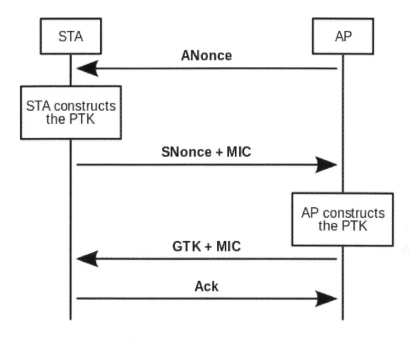

Figure 41 - Four-Way Handshake

The importance of the cryptographic nonces will become evident in the next chapter, where it is shown that they can be exploited to compromise some Wi-Fi encryption protocols.

CHAPTER 10. WIRELESS HACKING SETUP AND TOOLS

Wireless hacking requires specialized software tools and hardware due to the unique nature of wireless networks and their standard encryption schemes. The software tools are relatively easy to obtain and use, and come standard with Kali Linux packages. The wireless network adapters needed require a bit of research prior to acquisition, but are generally inexpensive and easy to find.

KALI LINUX TOOLS

Hacking for Beginners outlines a step-by-step procedure for cracking the password of a WEP-encrypted Wi-Fi network using Kali Linux. Chapter X of this book follows with a WPA/WPA2 attack using the same collection of tools. These tools are described in more detail here, along with the additional software that can be used to obscure the hacker's identity.

THE AIRCRACK SUITE

The *aircrack* suite is a collection of Linux-based open-source tools used for wireless network monitoring and penetration testing. All programs in the aircrack suite are executed at the Linux terminal command line. Although aircrack is used as a general term for the current suite, it has been officially titled ***aircrack-ng*** (a dash and "ng" suffix stands for "next generation" and is used to denote the branching of a software project with significant changes) since 2007. Aircrack-ng is also the name of one of the programs within the suite. The aircrack package is freely available and is included standard in Kali Linux.

The aircrack suite is written for the 802.11 Wi-Fi standard and can monitor or attack WEP and WPA/WPA2 encryption with the proper equipment. There are currently 16 programs in the suite that perform various sniffing, analysis, injection, decryption, or password cracking tasks, among other tasks.

The flagship program in the suite is the aircrack-ng encryption key cracking tool. This program uses different methods depending on whether it is cracking a WEP or a WPA/WPA2 key. The WEP key cracking method is based on a stream cipher attack which works by piecing together a large number of intercepted packets to form the key. This exploits an inherent weakness in initialization vectors for WEP. The stream cipher attack can be used in conjunction with a dictionary attack to exploit weak passwords more quickly. Aircrack-ng uses a dictionary attack to crack WPA/WPA2 as well, but this only works for significantly weak keys.

The **airmon-ng** tool is used to put the attacking machine's wireless adapter into a state called **monitor mode** (see next section). This step must be taken before any useful Wi-Fi monitoring can take place.

Airodump-ng is a wireless network packet sniffer, or network analyzer. It intercepts raw frames from the connected wireless adapter. Aircrack uses these frames to extract the initialization vectors that are needed to crack a WEP key.

Aireplay-ng is a packet injection tool that uses the connected wireless adapter to broadcast on the access point channel being attacked. Aireplay-ng can be used to deauthenticate clients on a network to increase traffic for airodump-ng to capture. Other attacks involving fake authentication and injection of forged packets can also be accomplished with aireplay-ng.

The programs described above are the most common and familiar aircrack tools. They can be used for most WEP and WPA/WPA2 cracking, denial-of-service, or injection attacks. The rest of the aircrack tools are listed in the table below with a brief description of their purpose.

airbase-ng	A tool for attacking wireless clients
airdecap-ng	Decrypts encrypted packets (when key is known)
airdecloak-ng	Filters any "cloaking" from captured WEP packets
airolib-ng	Maintains a database of passwords and keys for WPA/WPA2 cracking
airserv-ng	Allows other machines to use the connected wireless interface
airtun-ng	Creates a virtual tunnel connection for monitoring or injecting encrypted traffic
buddy-ng	A remote server used with easside-ng (see below)
easside-ng	Communicates with an uncracked, internet-connected, WEP-encrypted access point
ivstools	Extracts and merges initialization vectors from captured packets
packetforge-ng	Forges custom encrypted packets to be injected

MACCHANGER

One of the vulnerabilities of Wi-Fi is that signals are broadcast in all directions for anyone in range to detect. This is why encryption of data is so important in wireless networks. If someone is collecting, or "sniffing" the network traffic being broadcast on a particular channel, there is no way for that network's access point to know because monitoring is passive by nature. It is

important for hackers to remain inconspicuous, so passive attacks are always preferred when possible.

115

Unfortunately (for the hacker), many people are catching on to passive WEP attacks and WEP is being phased out. Most worthwhile wireless attacks will eventually require some degree of broadcasting or packet injection on the channel.

All IP packets must contain information about the source and destination nodes in the header, including the IP address and the MAC address. A hacker conducting a wireless attack is doing so through their own wireless network adapter, not through the internet, so any IP address information in a packet header sent by the hacker is ambiguous (in any case, it can be easily forged using aircrack tools listed in the previous section). Therefore, the origin of a wireless attack cannot be traced to a machine or location via the source IP like it can on the internet. However, all network interface cards come with a unique MAC address that indicates both the manufacturer and the individual device. Determined and well-funded law enforcement officials or security personnel can extract this identifier from suspicious packet headers and use it to attempt to identify the attacker. If the interface card was openly purchased by the hacker, the manufacturer could feasibly identify the merchant who sold the unit with that MAC address, the date and time of purchase, and the purchaser's identity from any financial trail left.

It is good practice, and a simple affair, thus, to alter the MAC address being broadcast in any packets during an attack. Although the MAC address is itself permanent in the hardware and cannot be changed, the address submitted into packet headers is easily forged with a simple (and free, open source) Linux tool called **macchanger**. With a single line, macchanger can alter the MAC address that is associated with a particular network interface to either a random address or an arbitrary one set by the user. Although a random MAC address or simplistic forgery (like 00:00:00:00:00:00 or FF:FF:FF:FF:FF:FF) will certainly hide the identity of an attacker, it can also make a packet appear suspicious to intrusion detection systems or network monitors. If a network does not recognize the manufacturer code on an incoming packet's MAC address, it could be designed to drop the packet or signal an alert.

To change a MAC address of an adapter in Kali Linux, it first must be taken out of service with the following command:

```
# ifconfig eth0 down
```

Where eth0 is the adapter to be altered. To change the MAC address of the adapter to a random address, use macchanger with a "-r" tag:

```
# macchanger -r eth0
```

A successful change will yield output similar to the following:

```
# Current MAC: 08:00:27:89:88:44
# Faked MAC:   95:45:0c:ad:64:94
```

Where the "Faked MAC" field contains the new, randomized hexadecimal MAC address now associated with the adapter. To change to a specified MAC address, use the "-m" tag:

```
# macchanger -m 00:03:77:7d:8a:05 eth0
```

Results:

```
# Current MAC: 95:45:0c:ad:64:94
# Faked MAC:   00:03:77:7d:8a:05
```

Finally, reconnect the adapter to use with the spoofed MAC address:

```
# ifconfig eth0 up
```

To forge the MAC address for a specific manufacturer, lists of prefixes associated with device manufacturers can be found online. Wireshark maintains a list at:

https://www.wireshark.org/tools/oui-lookup.html

WIRELESS ADAPTERS

Most computer hacking doesn't involve any special equipment beyond a computer, the necessary software tools (most of which are free), and some sort of network interface. However, wireless hacking, particularly for

the 802.11 Wi-Fi standard, typically requires a specialized wireless network adapter. In addition to monitor mode support (see below) a hacker may

118

require an external adapter with extended range or directional capability in order to reach a specific target.

MONITOR MODE

Under 802.11 Wi-Fi standard, network adapters can be operating at any one time in one of seven modes depending on the intend use of the device.

- *Master mode* – serving as the network access point
- *Managed mode* – a client on the network
- *Ad-hoc mode* – node with no access point
- *Mesh mode* – an alternative ad-hoc topology
- *Repeater mode* – rebroadcasting signals
- *Promiscuous mode* – sniffing associated traffic
- *Monitor mode* – sniffing all Wi-Fi traffic

Two modes of interest for hackers are promiscuous mode and monitor mode, both of which are used in network analysis. "Promiscuous" mode is a bit of a misnomer. Unlike the young lady in high school who went out with all the boys, a wireless adapter in promiscuous mode will not accept all packets that it detects. During promiscuous mode, the only packets captured are those with headers indicating that they have come from an access point to which the adapter is

currently associated. Conversely, a device in monitor (Radio Frequency Monitoring, or RFMON) mode is simply taking any Wi-Fi packets within its detectable range (An analogy would be the delivery of mail to your home. Ideally, you will only ever see mail or parcels that are addressed to your home. So you, in that case, are operating in promiscuous mode. However, at the post office, the people and machines that sort the mail can observe all mail passing through, and are therefore operating in monitor mode). This mode is necessary for cracking both WEP and WPA/WPA2 encryption because multiple encrypted packets on the protected network must be captured before decryption can be attempted. The airmon-ng tool is used to put a connected adapter into monitor mode. This single line process is shown in **Hacking for Beginners**.

For various reasons, not all wireless network adapters, drivers, or operating systems support all seven modes of Wi-Fi operation. In order to use the aircrack suite to its fullest potential, the hacker must obtain a wireless adapter that supports monitor mode. Most, if not all, internal wireless radios in desktops, laptops, and mobile devices *do not* support monitor mode. It is necessary to obtain a (typically external, USB) device with this capability before attacking a wireless network. This is not always a straightforward process, but the equipment is generally affordable and easy to obtain. The first step is to find a list of wireless adapter

controller chipsets that are supported by your intended operating system. This list will change periodically and supported chips will come and go - the best way to find a working list is through internet searches and forums.

The following is a partial list of wireless chipsets that support monitor mode within Kali Linux as of 2017.

- Atheros AR9271
- Ralink RT3070 and RT3572
- Realtek 8187L Wireless G and RTL8812AU

Once you know which chipsets are supported by your operating system, it becomes relatively easy to search for a network adapter that features one of those chipsets. A common manufacturer of external USB wireless adapters that feature monitor mode chipsets in Kali Linux is Alfa Network, Inc.

CHAPTER 11. HACKING WPA2 WI-FI ENCRYPTION

Understanding the basic operations involved in Wi-Fi communication, as presented in Chapter 9, is the first step in exploiting its vulnerabilities. The book *Hacking for Beginners* provides a good introduction to the various wireless encryption protocols and open-source tools for attacking networks, and steps through one of the more rudimentary hacks. This chapter follows by assessing more advanced protocols and their vulnerabilities. It's important to remember that once a hacking procedure becomes well known and is put into common use, it usually isn't very long until the vulnerability is fixed or the target in question is abandoned altogether. A great hacker should never be complacent and should try to stay informed about the latest attacks.

Wi-Fi hacking lends itself particularly well to practicing hacks safely. The best way to become familiar and proficient at different Wi-Fi attacks is to simply exploit one's own network. With access to a wireless router, the hacker can set the encryption protocol, change password lengths and complexity, or make other changes that affect security. Hacking one's own Wi-Fi network and then tweaking various parameters to counter is the best way to become an expert hacker in a consequence-free environment.

WI-FI ENCRYPTION PROTOCOLS

Hacking for Beginners provides a brief history and overview of standard encryption protocols from the inception of Wi-Fi. This chapter will review some of that information in light of more advanced concepts, but will emphasize the most recent standards and technology – which provide more challenging targets.

WEP

The first encryption protocol used for wireless networking was Wired Equivalent Privacy (*WEP)*. The name derives from the fact that the original authors of the Wi-Fi standard recognized that additional measures were needed to secure wireless data transmissions that were being overtly broadcast – something that was not an issue with cable-connected networks. A method was needed to bridge the gap in confidentiality between wired and wireless media.

Unfortunately (but fortunately for hackers!), it didn't take long before inherent weaknesses in WEP were discovered. WEP uses a one-time "initialization vector", or *IV* (similar to a nonce) in its authentication handshakes. This vector is appended to the shared key, but is sent unencrypted because it is intended to only be used once. However, because the IV length is so short, it will naturally reappear at random intervals if there is sufficient traffic. Therefore, hackers simply need to passively capture data packets on the target channel and recover a portion of the key every time the IV reappears. The heavier the traffic on the target network, the faster the entire key can be recovered (see Figure 42).

Hacking for Beginners outlines the procedure for exploiting a WEP-encrypted Wi-Fi network. A special wireless adapter is needed for the procedure whose chipset supports "monitor mode". This equipment is relatively inexpensive and easy to find. Kali Linux features all the software needed to perform the hack, including *airmon-ng*, *airodump-ng*, and *aircrack-ng*. Improvements to WEP, including a larger IV size, have increased the time it takes to hack a WEP-encrypted network, but the vulnerability remains. Many newer wireless routers no longer include WEP as an encryption setting due to its insecurity, and it is generally recommended not to be used to secure a network unless it is necessary for support of some legacy clients. Hacking WEP is a good way, however, for hackers to get their feet wet and become familiar with some of the common tools used for wireless exploitation.

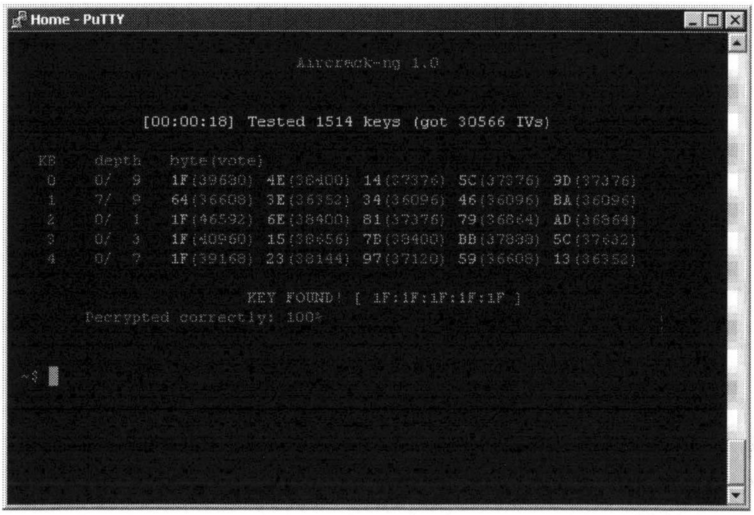

Figure 42 - A Successfully Decrypted Wi-Fi Key (aircrack-ng.org)

WPA

The response to the security vulnerabities of WEP was the development of an entirely new encryption protocol called WPA2, which will be described below. However, implementation of WPA2 required new router hardware to be manufactured and distributed. For equipment that could not support WPA2, the stop-gap measure of WPA could be implemented as a significant, if temporary, improvement upon WEP. Wi-Fi Protected Access (**WPA**) was a software implementation that improved the security of wireless communication through use of a firmware update to WEP-enabled wireless interface cards.

Instead of using a unique initialization vector appended

to a shared key, WPA dynamically changes the entire 128-bit encryption key on a per-packet basis. In addition, WPA began implementing the message authentication code (MAC), described in the previous chapter, to prevent the reuse of old packets. These procedures are referred to collectively as the Temporal Key Integrity Protocol (*TKIP*).

Despite the improvements that WPA provided over WEP, it was inevitably compromised by hackers – although by more advanced means than that of WEP. WPA attacks, in contrast to the passivity of WEP exploitation, required hackers to transmit packets into the target network channel in what is known as *packet injection*. Packet injection can be accomplished using another tool in the aircrack suite called *aireplay-ng*. Since WPA2 has been available for over a decade now and is considered the most secure protocol, WPA is no longer supported or recommended for use.

WPA2

Wi-Fi Protected Access II (*WPA2*) is the current standard encryption protocol for Wi-Fi networks. There are three types of key distribution methods for WPA2, depending on the type and size of the network:

1. Pre-Shared Key (*WPA-PSK*) – for home and small-office networks
2. Enterprise – for large and corporate networks (requires an authentication server)

3. Wi-Fi Protected Setup (**WPS**) – a simplified, but insecure method

The book will confine discussion to WPA-PSK and is referring to that system when mentioning WPA2.

WPA2 improved upon the weak TKIP encryption of WPA by adopting the Advanced Encryption Standard (**AES**).

HACKING WPA2

Despite the tremendous improvements in security offered by WPA2 over WEP and WPA, it has its share of exploitable vulnerabilities. If users employ weak passwords, their networks are susceptible to dictionary attacks and other brute-force methods – even under WPA2. Although WPA2 cannot as yet be compromised by trivial, passive exploits like WEP, hackers have been busy probing for weaknesses. Several attacks have emerged over the years of varying complexity. Often, Wi-Fi standards have countered with updates and various patches.

AIRCRACK

The procedure outlined here is intended to build upon the skills learned in the passive WEP attack explained in **Hacking for Beginners**, and uses the aircrack suite included in Kali Linux. This attack assumes that the target system has a weak (using common words) or relatively short password, otherwise it would take prohibitively long to execute. As with any attack, not all equipment and software is the same and not everything will always go as planned, so the reader is encouraged to refer to multiple sources for information and troubleshooting. To attack WPA/WPA2

1) View all Wi-Fi traffic in range while in "monitor mode" (set by airmon-ng) using airodump-ng.

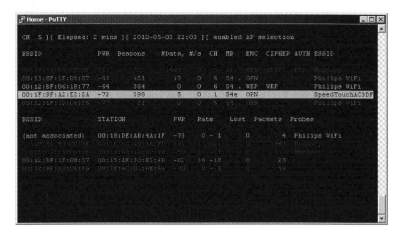

Figure 43 - airodump-ng results

Live W-Fi Traffic on Several Routers (.aircrack-ng.org)

2) Choose a target Wi-Fi network that is using WPA or WPA2 encryption and make a note of the name (ESSID) and network address (BSSID in the form XX:XX:XX:XX:XX:XX).

3) Restart **airodump-ng** to begin capturing network traffic from the specific network that you are targeting:

```
~$ airodump-ng -c CH --bssid XX:XX:XX:XX:XX:XX -w psk
ath0
```

where CH is the channel for target BSSID MAC address XX:XX:XX:XX:XX:XX and ath0 is the monitor mode enabled adapter.

4) Deploy the aireplay-ng script to "deauthenticate" (see the previous chapter) any clients that are currently connected to the target network. This forces a new handshake and speeds up the cracking process.

```
# aireplay-ng -0 1 -a XX:XX:XX:XX:XX:XX -c
CC:CC:CC:CC:CC:CC ath0
```

where CC:CC:CC:CC:CC:CC MAC address of the deauthentication target.

5) Run aircrack-ng to run through a dictionary list and attempt to crack the pre-shared key:

```
# aircrack-ng -w password.lst -b XX:XX:XX:XX:XX:XX
psk*.cap
```

where password.lst is a dictionary file in the local path.

A successful WPA/WPA2 dictionary attack will yield output of the pre-shared key (Figure 7), and the resulting password!.

Figure 44 - A cracked WPA2 password (itfellover.com)

THE NONCE "KRACK"

Although deauthentication via packet injection can significantly speed up cracking of a WPA/WPA2 key, it is easily thwarted by simply using greater password complexity. Dictionary attacks are effectively useless against long, random character strings. More advanced methods are needed to break a well-implemented WPA2 network.

Quite recently, researchers discovered a vulnerability in the 4-way WPA2 handshake process and presented a paper of their findings at a technical conference. The procedure is known as the Key Reinstallation AttaCK (**KRACK**). This attack exploits the use of the cryptographic nonce (introduced in the previous chapter) that is issued during authentication. Although by their very nature, nonces are only supposed to be used once and discarded, there is no mechanism in the

WPA2 protocol to ensure this. Therefore, if the handshake process can be manipulated in such a way as to force the reissue of a nonce, information about the key can be gleaned by hackers.

Recall that in step 3 of the 4-way handshake, the access point sends a final message to the client and awaits acknowledgement. It is not unusual, especially in wireless communication where signal interference is significant, for packets to be lost in transmission. If the AP does not receive an ACK from the client, it will therefore resend handshake message number 3 until it is acknowledged or times out. Each time the client gets this message, it is reusing the nonce until the handshake is complete! KRACK works by intercepting message 3 transmissions from the AP and spoofing the loss of packets by retransmitting them to the client in order to force the reuse of the Snonce.

The important thing to remember about this attack is that it simply allows the hacker to decrypt the contents of client packets, revealing potentially sensitive information. It does *not*, however, crack the password to the network itself. The procedure is advanced and multifaceted, requiring some scripts to be written to conduct the attack. A demonstration can be found in the following video:

https://youtu.be/Oh4WURZoR98

Figure 8 shows the contents of a packet that was successfully decrypted using KRACK procedures. In this demonstration, the packet (i.e. "frame") contained user form data submitted to a website.

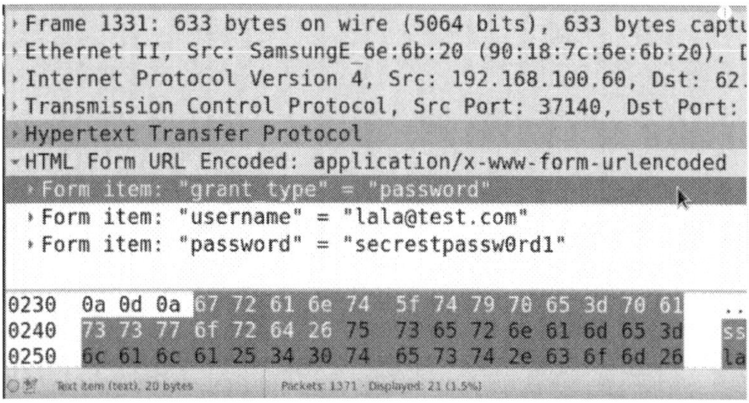

```
▸ Frame 1331: 633 bytes on wire (5064 bits), 633 bytes captu
▸ Ethernet II, Src: SamsungE_6e:6b:20 (90:18:7c:6e:6b:20), [
▸ Internet Protocol Version 4, Src: 192.168.100.60, Dst: 62.
▸ Transmission Control Protocol, Src Port: 37140, Dst Port:
▸ Hypertext Transfer Protocol
▾ HTML Form URL Encoded: application/x-www-form-urlencoded
  ▸ Form item: "grant_type" = "password"
  ▸ Form item: "username" = "lala@test.com"
  ▸ Form item: "password" = "secrestpassw0rd1"

0230  0a 0d 0a 67 72 61 6e 74  5f 74 79 70 65 3d 70 61   ..
0240  73 73 77 6f 72 64 26 75  73 65 72 6e 61 6d 65 3d   ss
0250  6c 61 6c 61 25 34 30 74  65 73 74 2e 63 6f 6d 26   la
```
Text item (text), 20 bytes   Packets: 1371 · Displayed: 21 (1.5%)

Figure 45 - A successful KRACK attack (www.krackattacks.com)

132

Chapter 12. Wireless Routers and Network Exploitation

Gaining access to a wireless network is an accomplishment (one that will be more challenging as Wi-Fi security improves), but it is only the first step toward more productive goals. When attacking a wireless network, a hacker has typically any of three goals in mind:

1. Gaining access to a client on the network
2. Gaining access to the access point
3. Executing denial of service

The latter goal, denial of service, does not necessarily require access to the network, but can be accomplished using the same suite of tools. This chapter will discuss some aspects of wireless router security and outline the tools that are used to analyze and exploit the members of a network.

Router Security

Breaking the encryption of a wireless network gives you access to the network itself, but not necessarily to the connected nodes. Clients and access points will have their own security measures that the hacker must contend with. The wireless routers that are typically used as access points in a Wi-Fi LAN are intended only for administrative access and have built-in security. Routers also have certain vulnerabities which, when exploited, can give hackers free reign over the network. Having access to the router gives hackers the ability to change encryption protocols, intercept privileged data, or deny access to legitimate users.

ADMINISTRATIVE PASSWORDS

The configuration software of a wireless router is typically in the form of firmware embedded on the device. This program, called a gateway, is accessed through a client web interface directly to the IP address of the router. An authenticated user accesses the interface when connected to the network (regardless of any internet connection) by typing the router's IP address into the address bar of their web browser. The router address is usually a standard format, which can vary by the age of the device, and will be included in the product documentation or on a label attached to the device itself. Two common router IPv4 address formats are:

192.168.X.X
10.0.X.X

The web application will greet users with a username and password prompt on the home screen (see figure X), but some gateways may also include some general information about the network and any connected clients.

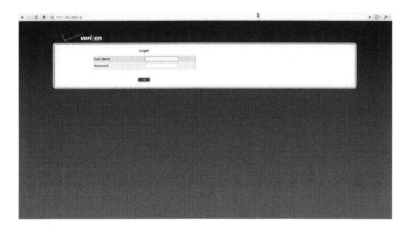

Figure 46 - Wi-Fi Router Login

The default administrative username and password to access the router is included in the product documentation or on the device. Many routers, particularly older ones, have a standard username and password across all models so that administrators can reset the device to an easily known password if they forget the one they set. This is a vulnerability if the hacker has physical access to the router. Also, if the user neglects to change the default password, the default for that model of router is freely available to hackers online. In many cases, default logins are so common and uniform that they are quickly guessed. Some common combinations have traditionally been:

username: admin
password: <blank>

username: admin
password: admin

username: <blank>
password: admin

username: admin
password: password

Comprehensive databases exists online with router logins sorted by brand and model. One such website is:

http://www.routerpasswords.com/

CRACKING WPS WITH AIRCRACK AND BULLY

One operating mode that has been added to the Wi-Fi standard in recent years is wireless protected setup (WPS). The purpose of WPS is to facilitate sign-on by wireless clients through the use of a WPS button on the router that pairs the client device with the router, or alternatively through an 8-digit PIN code. The underlying WPA/WPA2 encryption (WPS is not available with WEP) is still being used, but clients use WPA to connect without needing the encryption key. This presents some clear vulnerabilities in the security of the router. Even if a router is using an encryption key that is strong enough to thwart known cracking methods, if WPS is enabled, a hacker need only use basic brute-force methods to obtain the WPS pin in a reasonable amount of time. Furthermore, in some devices, even if the router is configured to connect with a WPS button, the network can still be hacked with the routers default WPS pin.

Router manufacturers have caught on to this vulnerability and have attempted to address it in new hardware and in firmware updates, but the problem remains in many older, unpatched access points. Kali Linux features a brute-force WPS attack script known as *bully* that works with the aircrack suite and a monitor mode capable wireless adapter to break both the WPS pin, subsequently revealing the encryption password. Sometimes this can be done in a matter of hours.

After placing the connected Wi-Fi adapter of the attacking machine in monitor mode, start airodump-ng to begin collecting packets, using the procedure outlined in this book and in *Hacking for Beginners*.

After selecting a target network from the airodump screen (it must be one that you know is vulnerable or this procedure won't produce results), run bully to attack the PIN:

```
# bully mon0 -b <XX:XX:XX:XX:XX:XX> -e <ESSID> -c
<CH>
```

where <XX:XX:XX:XX:XX:XX>, <ESSID>, and <CH> are the target network's MAC address (BSSID), ESSID, and channel, respectively. After running for the necessary length of time, bully will simply output the WPS PIN and

WPA/WPA2 encryption key to the command terminal.

NETWORK MAPPING WITH NMAP.

After gaining access to a wireless network, the next major step for the hacker is to probe for any exploitable client vulnerabilities. First, however, a bird's-eye view of the network and its connected clients is useful for identifying potential targets. It should be of no surprise that Kali Linux comes with a free, open source network mapping application. Network Mapper, or **nmap**, scans a connected network by "pinging" nodes on the network with special packets that are designed to elicit a response from the hosts. Nmap analyzes the response packets and methodically builds a "map" of the network by discovering the hosts, scanning their ports, and determining the type and versions of the operating systems running on each device.

A simple way to get acquainted with nmap and practice network mapping is to use it on one's own network. Like other Linux commands, nmap has a number of options that can be appended to the command to specify desired functions. The '-sn' option conducts a simple scan for open hosts on the network. The following example:

nmap -sn 10.0.0.*

Cycles through all IP addresses in the provided domain and reports the MAC addresses of any open hosts, including the manufacturers associated with known MAC addresses. Figure 47 shows the results on a wireless home network.

Figure 47 - nmap results

A cursory look at the output reveals devices that can be assumed are smart phones, tablets, routers, printers and connected appliances. Some of the manufacturer names refer to the network adapters of what are possibly computers.

Although nmap itself is a command line application and produces text output, its results can be parsed by companion applications that provide a more visual representation of the network. The **zenmap** application included in Kali Linux can produce a graphical network topology (Figure 48) using nmap as a back end.

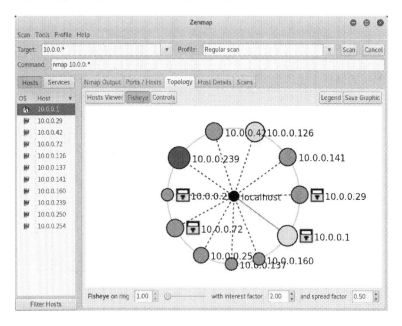

Figure 48 - zenmap results

The "-O" (capital letter O) option in nmap can be used determine the operating system running on a target host. This information is useful in planning an exploit. Running an OS scan on target 10.0.0.1 reveals its open ports and a Linux-based OS.

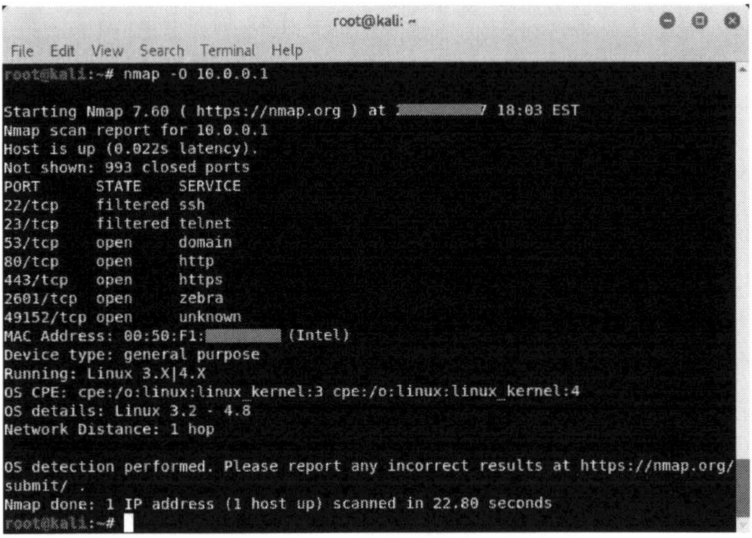

Figure 49 - OS Scanning in nmap

A wide array of nmap options allow the user to control how much or how little information to collect and reveal on a scan.

It is important to remember that using nmap is *not* a passive activity – it works by exchanging packets with target nodes. Some machines are equipped to detect when they are being scanned and to raise an alert, collect header information from the incoming packets, or block the suspicious origin IP address.

METASPLOIT

Metasploit is one of the most powerful tools in the arsenal of serious hackers. Metasploit provides a framework for detecting and exploiting vulnerabilities in target ports. It makes use of a constantly updated database of known system vulnerabilities and their associated exploits. As of 2017 Metasploit features over 1600 exploits (and growing).

Metasploit requires an external interface to run. There are several choices of interfaces that can run Metasploit, some of which manage other applications as well. The **msfconsole** (Metasploit Framework Console) application, available in Kali Linux, is a standard interface for running Metasploit. To launch:

Figure 50 - msfconsole

A useful feature of msfconsole is that other tools, like nmap, can be run within the interface – although sometimes with different syntax than in the Linux command terminal. To run nmap on a selected target:

```
msf > db_nmap <options> <target ip>
```

After identifying a target, you can search the metasploit database for vulnerabilities in the operating system or open service identified in your scans:

```
msf > search <keyword>
```

where <keyword> identifies the target service or application:

Figure 51 - metasploit Vulnerability Search

Known vulnerabilities are listed and described along with their respective discovery dates.

143

CHAPTER 13. WIRELESS DENIAL OF SERVICE

Denial of Service (DoS) attacks, introduced in principle in *Hacking for Beginners*, are attempts to prevent legitimate users from accessing services or resources on a given host. Reasons for DoS attacks range from general mischief and social or political activism to the more serious activities of blackmail or state-sponsored electronic warfare. DoS attacks are comparatively easy to execute because they don't necessarily require access to the target system and therefore don't involve complicated decryption or the injection of payloads. As a result, these attacks can be launched across the internet from multiple anonymous locations, many of which may be hijacked hosts who have become unwitting participants. This is known as Distributed Denial of Service (DDoS) and is very difficult and costly to prevent.

Wireless denial of service differs from traditional "wire line" DoS attacks in that the attacker (at least, the end-point attacking host) must be within radio-frequency range of the target access point. Wireless DoS attacks can be executed by jamming the Wi-Fi signal on the target channel or by forcing the access point to repeatedly deauthenticate legitimate associated clients.

These are not passive attacks and may require care to obfuscate the source of offending packets.

There is some disagreement as to whether denial of service is technically "hacking", since the attacker is not actually gaining access to resources. Regardless, DoS attacks involve the same set of skills and tools as other types of hacking and results in unintended system behavior. As much as any other type of attack, security professionals must understand how they are conducted in order to guard against them. Also, deauth attacks are often a precursor to more intrusive activities and are used to force clients onto compromised access points.

DEAUTHENTICATION ATTACKS

Chapter 9 discusses the handshake process with which Wi-Fi networks authenticate clients. This process involves a multi-step exchange of packets between the authenticating agent (typically an access point or router) and the client. One of the responsibilities of the access point (AP) is to reauthenticate clients who have been temporarily disconnected (a common occurrence in wireless networks), which it does by prompting the client to acknowledge (ACK) receipt of the initial handshake packet.

A deauthentication (deauth) attack works by sending a stream of packets to both the AP and the client. The AP and the client respond with ACK packets that are out of context for a standard handshake procedure (Figure 9). As long as this attack is sustained, the client under attack is unable to be properly authenticated on the network. This is an example of a man-in-the-middle attack (see **Hacking for Beginners**). It only requires spoofed packets and does not require the attacking machine to be part of the network or have the encryption key.

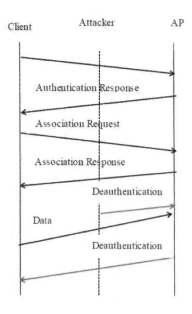

Figure 52 - Deauthentication Attack (opensourceforu.com)

"DEAUTH" ATTACKS WITH AIRCRACK

A simple Wi-Fi deauth attack can be launched using the aircrack suite and a suitable wireless adapter that supports monitor mode.

146

Using the procedure outlined in previous chapters, put the connected Wi-Fi adapter of the attacking machine in monitor mode and start airodump-ng to begin collecting packets. You may also spoof your MAC address with macchanger for some anonymity. Choose a client on the airodump list that you wish to deny service. For this attack you will need the BSSID (MAC address) of both the client and the associated AP. The aireplay-ng packet injection command is used for deauthentication:

```
# aireplay-ng -0 1 -a 00:14:6C:XX:XX:XX -c
00:0F:B5:XX:XX:XX ath0
```

Where -0 tells the program to inject deauth packets. The "1" is the number of times the procedure is to be run, sending 64 packets to each node. The higher the number, the longer the attack will last. A "0" will cause the attack to repeat until manually halted. The -a option is followed by the AP's BSSID and the -c by the client's BSSID. "ath0" is the attacking wifi adapter.

CHAPTER 14. CONCLUSION

ETHICS

Hacking for Beginners discusses the different "hats" of hacking - the black, the white, and the grey. The black hat is the stereotypical idea of how most in society conceive hackers to be - the one who wants unauthorized access to the property or information of another. The white hat is the "good guy" - the one learning the tricks of the trade in order to prevent the exploitation of assets or track down offenders. The grey hat is a bit of a hybrid, they use their hacking skills (although without the prior knowledge or authorization of the owners) to expose weaknesses in systems so that those systems can be strengthened. Regardless of the motivations of any individuals, the knowledge base and general toolkit remain the same. Hacking requires an understanding of how computing equipment communicates on various levels, what vulnerabilities lie in both machines and networks, and how those vulnerabilities are exploited. This knowledge takes time, practice, study, and discipline to attain, and it is not something that everyday people are familiar with. As a result, skilled hackers have the ability to either inflict or prevent quite a bit of damage on individuals, organizations, and society.

Each hacker should thus adopt some code of ethics to guide them. Even black hats will have some line that they will not cross in carrying out their attacks. Law enforcement is becoming very serious about information security and preventing pervasive attacks on individual identities, on commerce, and on government institutions. Laws and enforcement vary by location, but any hacker - black, white, or grey - should have a full understanding of the risks they are taking. This is especially true of beginning hackers who don't have the experience to either hide their tracks or to prevent collateral damage. An attack that is conducted improperly could erase or corrupt information, or cause other unintended consequences. That is why it is important to practice skills on one's on systems in an isolated "sandbox" until gaining enough confidence to attack another system.

MAINTAINING THE HACKER'S EDGE

There is a perpetual race going on between the hacker community and the information security community. When vulnerability is discovered, it tends to spread wisely and rapidly as evidenced by the WPA Krack attack described in Chapter X. Security personnel try to keep up by constantly making patches or upgrades to protect systems. Hackers must constantly hone their craft and push limits in order to maintain an edge. Like any skill, hacker skills dwindle if not in regular use. Furthermore, the landscape in computer security is in constant flux. The open source nature of most hacking tools means that there are frequent changes in functionality and syntax that must be kept up with. Vulnerabilities are published and patched on a near daily basis, and encryption standards are being pushed very hard to provide better security against attacks. So to maintain an edge and to have a reasonable chance of becoming a successful hacker, one should do the following:

1. Maintain current versions of all operating systems, scripts, tools, and programming environments

2. Practice skills on a regular basis, on a sandboxed environment, with emphasis on improving both speed and anonymity

3. Periodically probe their own system and adopt the appropriate security measures

4. Have a daily or weekly reading cycle on both offensive and defensive security developments (magazines, journals, web articles, message boards, dark web hacker communities, etc.) Chapter Text

About the Author

Alan T. Norman is a proud, savvy, and ethical hacker from San Francisco City. After receiving a Bachelor's of Science at Stanford University. Alan now works for a mid-size Informational Technology Firm in the heart of SFC. He aspires to work for the United States government as a security hacker, but also loves teaching others about the future of technology. Alan firmly believes that the future will heavily rely computer "geeks" for both security and the successes of companies and future jobs alike. In his spare time, he loves to analyze and scrutinize everything about the game of basketball.

CRYPTOCURRENCY MINING BONUS BOOK

FIND THE LINK TO THE BONUS BOOK BELOW

www.erdpublishing.com/cryptocurrency-mining-bonus/

OTHER BOOKS BY ALAN T. NORMAN

Mastering Bitcoin for Starters

Cryptocurrency Investing Bible
http://mybook.to/cryptoBible

Blockchain Technology Explained

http://mybook.to/BlockchainExplained

Hacking: Computer Hacking Beginners Guide

http://mybook.to/hacking

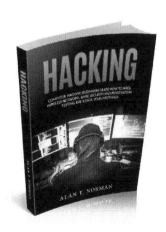

Hacking: How to Make Your Own Keylogger in C++ Programming Language

http://mybook.to/keylogger

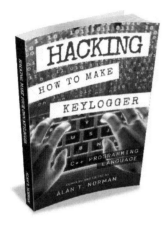

ONE LAST THING…

DID YOU ENJOY THE BOOK?

IF SO, THEN LET ME KNOW BY LEAVING A REVIEW ON AMAZON! Reviews are the lifeblood of independent authors. I would appreciate even a few words and rating if that's all you have time for

IF YOU DID NOT LIKE THIS BOOK, THEN PLEASE TELL ME! Email me at alannormanit@gmail.com and let me know what you didn't like! Perhaps I can change it. In today's world a book doesn't have to be stagnant, it can improve with time and feedback from readers like you. You can impact this book, and I welcome your feedback. Help make this book better for everyone!

24765027R00090

Printed in Poland
by Amazon Fulfillment
Poland Sp. z o.o., Wrocław